RENOUNCE IT
NOW!

Overcome Brainwashing, Spiritual Manipulation

and

Witchcraft Today!

Mya Chavis
Enterprise™

Intrigue, Attract, Inspire

Mya A Chavis

Written by Mya A Chavis
Edited by Casey Kaiser

www.myachavis.com

TABLE OF CONTENTS

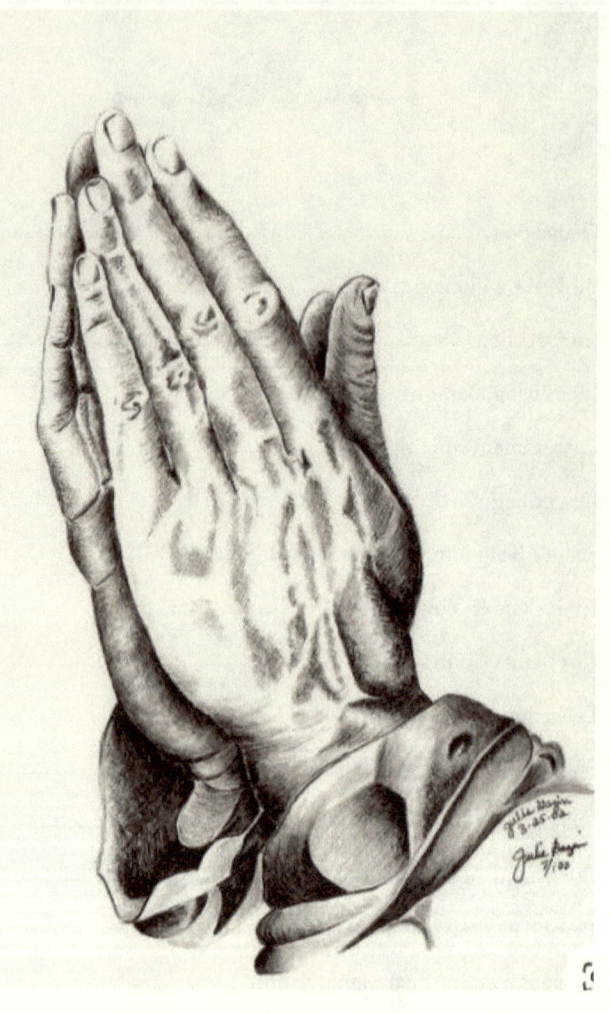

DEDICATION

"I Dedicate this book to the late great Annie Mae Ecclesiastics Chavis, my grandmother. The best whoever did it and the best demon slayer, whoever slayed". Also, to Darren Shephard who stringently encouraged me to write a "Spiritual Book".

Mya A Chavis

"For the weapons of our warfare are not carnal but mighty in God for pulling down strongholds".

2 Corinthians 10:4 NKJV

Jeremiah 29:11

BIBLICAL CAUTIONING

"This I say, therefore, and testify in the Lord, that you should no longer walk <u>as the rest of</u> the Gentiles walk, in the futility of their mind, having their understanding darkened, being alienated from the life of God, because of the ignorance that is in them, because of the blindness of their heart;"

Ephesians 4 17-18

John 3:16

INTRODUCTION

Spiritual Manipulation and Witchcraft are evil practices widely prevalent in today's society. Although quietly swept under the radar, they are being practiced in plain sight proactively everywhere, including but not limited to the shows you watch on television, the music that you listen to, the movies that you watch and stream on the internet. Institutions (educational and theological) that you may have willingly enlisted. It is imperative, that we are able to intelligently, decipher, discern, renounce and reject these unclean dark spirit forces, (especially) the believer.

The only way to truly and effectively overcome and confidently be delivered from such occurrences of evil spirits is that the spirit must be bound and the warring spirit of the Lord must be loosed. This book may not supply you with all the answers but it will definitely provide a scriptural foundation for "identifying and overcoming" spiritual manipulation and witchcraft. During quiet time seeking and chasing Yahweh. God called me to write this simple but impactfully powerful manual sharing what it is and what the Bible says about overcoming gross immaterial attacks of spiritual coercions utilizing modern-day occult practices, otherwise known as "witchcraft " and her twin "spiritual manipulation".

As regular people, Christians and "End Time Believers", it is imperative that we are able to discern spiritually, identify and renounce both crucial components of Spiritual Manipulation and Witchcraft. These immaterial appointments rarely introduce themselves as they intentionally are. These evil forces will more than likely never introduce themselves by saying, hi! my name is demon. Unfortunately, it doesn't work that way. It is absolutely crucial to use common sense, wisdom, and knowledge before willfully accepting what the devil tries to force down your throat. It could be a matter of life, death or potentially your soul.

Being deceived is not part of the plans and purposes of God or his kingdom. It is written that we ought to *"be sober, be vigilant; because your adversary the devil, as a roaring lion, roams around seeking whom he may devour."* **1 Peter 5:8** "There is nothing new under the sun. There is no situation surprising to God, nothing you pronounce to him will catch him off guard. Your road map or GPS through life should be found within the 66 books of the Gospel of God's word. Especially concerning the scriptures that enforce wisdom, trumping and overturning deception pertaining to the world ruler of wickedness himself, lucifer. The original survival guide to life is the Bible. Nothing can supersede its laws nor his commandments on how we are to live the complicated life. Being mindful of God's laws and presets he sat before us as instructions as to how, we should live our life on earth, even today and keep us guarded against ignorance to spiritual attacks, traps and devices.

Ephesians 4 17-18 "This I say, therefore, and testify in the Lord, that you should no longer walk as the rest of the Gentiles walk, in the futility of their mind, <u>having their understanding darkened, being alienated from the life of God, because of the ignorance that is in them,</u> because of the blindness of their heart."

If we as believers are not mindful and discerned in the spirit realm, we stand as open targets, leaving ourselves susceptible, vulnerable, easily able to be deceived, manipulated or taken captive into a debased, defeated lifestyle of "Spiritual Slavery" being entrapped in perpetual rigorous circumstances beyond our own control. **Colossians 2:8** "*See to it that no one takes you captive through hollow and deceptive philosophy, which depends on human tradition and the elemental spiritual forces of this world rather than on Christ*". As believers, we must be able to realize & recognize the stealth tricks and traps of the Kingdom of Darkness, or else, we can be devoured. Therefore, I won't bore you with drawn-out philosophies, theories or my overly enhanced vocabulary. This is a "Scripture Based Guide" to keep regular people, Christians and "End Time Believers" alike, awake, aware, and soberly diligent to schemes of the evil worldly antagonists of this age. To those who are fed up and ready to take a stand against the devil's scams pertaining to Spiritual Manipulation and her twin Witch-Craft. What you don't know can and will hurt you.

James 2:19

IDENTIFYING DEMONS

Merriam-Webster Dictionary describes the word "demon" as being a source or agent of evil, harm, distress, or AKA an "evil spirit". They are evil supernatural beings that are devout followers and worshipers of satan himself. Most demons are extremely persistent, zealous, skillful, charming and diligent in achieving satan's plans to reform, recruit and brainwash as many souls as possible to join him for permanent torment, in the kingdom of darkness otherwise known as Sheol or Hell.

Originally, demons had been angels of heaven, that were later evicted from God's heavenly estate, now known as fallen angels or hellish- imps (**Revelation 9:1**). They joined forces with Satan otherwise known as (Belial, Behemoth, Beelzebub) to oppose God, deceive God's people and wreak havoc upon the Kingdom of God on earth as well as in heaven (**Revelation 12:4**)(**Revelation 12:9**). To detour, frustrate and stop the plans and purposes of God's kingdom. They form a regimented

satanic army to torment, irritate, frustrate, chain you to
inequity, bound your soul and your mind to evil and evil
treacherous acts that would only please Lucifer. Such acts
include mass shootings, violence against children and the
elderly, sexual violence and theft. They are treacherous
evil spirits who possess unlimited sources of wickedness,
appearing in all forms of flesh, human, paranormal and
animal. The lies they conjure up come directly from
satan's play- book itself. Their main objective is to create
harm, distress, and ruin among God's people, and the
Anointed First Creation in all of the earth as well as his
places of worship. Especially God's heavenly kingdom!

They are regimented forces of evil vowed to and
enlisted into the regimented ordinance, government and
army of lucifer, the prince of darkness, deceiver, serpent,
accuser of the brethren. The Anti-Christ Himself.

"You are of your father the devil, and
the desires of your father you want to
do. He was a murderer from the
beginning, and does not stand in the
truth, because there is no truth in him.
When he speaks a lie, he speaks from
his own resources, for he is a liar and
the father of it.
John 44 8

Luke 10:18, John 8:44, Matthew 25:41 .

1 Peter 5:8-9 , **Isaiah 14:12**. Being deceived by the devil they joined forces with him. Willfully, they abandoned their heavenly tenancy, an irreplaceable royal estate intricately constructed for them by Jehovah.

Revelation 20:1-3, **Genesis 3:14**, Their failed attempt to overthrow God and his Heavenly Kingdom was a failed mission that did not succeed but cost them eternity! Now they roam the earth with a regimented allegiance to the devil, their commander and chief, doing his will and his way, which outright rebelliously contradicts and opposes the will of the only wise God, Yahweh. Ignorance is their most "viable tool of deception". They count on and depend on the believer or Babe in Christ to not know their word, and not know how to launch and effectually use their spiritual weaponry.

Through violence, hatred, outbursts of wrath, disobedience, sexual sin, murder, idolatry, jealousy, envy, sadism, satanic worship, witchcraft, voodoo, hoodoo, divination, lukewarmness, wishy-washiness, incest, addiction, soul wounds, perversion, ungodly soul ties, sorcery, hypnotism through beats and music, hexes, oaths to secret societies, confusion, spells, greed, the love & passion for money, wounded spirits and silent generational curses; they are very active in pursuing their wicked luciferin agenda.

Their main focal goals are to deceive as many as possible so that they will join them as everlasting company in their permanent fiery inferno. They outwardly toil with the believer's faith and inject into the mind, much confusion and ill- advised "fruitless theology" that is often over-saturated with worldly carnality, and is not of God's word to invoke utter doubt and mass confusion. We do not serve a God of confusion; his scriptural precepts are both logical and precise. Desperate, they stand by, hoping that the target will turn against God, backslide and abandoned their faith, through conformity, ignorance, confusion and atheistic, fleshly-worldly thinking.

Lastly, demons are dispersed into the air and all throughout the earth to disturb the plans and the purposes that God has set forth for his people to receive their heavenly inheritance which is "Salvation", our blessed assurance in Jesus Christ the "Promised Risen Messiah".

The enemy satan and his demons know two things confidently, they know Christ is real, and that he is the real "Son of God". It is written in scripture that even the demons tremble and believe. **James 2:19** "You believe that there is one God. You do well. Even the demons believe—and tremble"! Demons also understand the cost of sin is an eternal everlasting death! The gift of life is salvation. Christ defeated all 6 realms of the kingdom of darkness Aka "Sheol", to be exact that is; death, hell, the grave, abyss, the lake, and perdition.

In pursuance to making it through these difficult last days and times you must be able to discern demons,

13

witchcraft and their main weapons of offense which are (control and deceitful manipulation) against God's people, his church and his holy word. Deception, spiritual manipulation, and witchcraft (viable & subliminal) are wicked utensils that have been used to dupe individuals out of their salvation for thousands of years prior. It's vital to identify what they are and what they stand for. It is utterly crucial to renounce any involvement of, alliance, allegiances or ungodly soul ties (knowing and unknowingly). Bind evil spirits, rebuke their blasphemy and attacks. Loose the powerful army of God to fight and win this battle on your behalf so that you might be loosed from any chains of infirmity. Be mindful, this is a supernatural fight fought in the supernatural. The invisible war is very real. Overcoming won't be easy and may encompass some sleepless nights, tear-soaked pillows, revelations of fake friends and perhaps even faker family members. It is imperative to note and not be taken by surprise at the fact that on occasion the devil uses the people closest to you preferably long before he uses your obvious enemies. Stay awake and stay on guard to peoples' actions, energy and motives for they won't lie. Pay close attention to the revelation of false prophets and counterfeit preachers "fronting in the name of Jesus". Sadly, it may be revealed people who you thought were in your corner were really on the devil's side the entire time. Don't fret, just know that often those "Planted Judases" are all part of the plan to overcome. This is not a battle for the gullible, naive, weak or faint of heart. One has to have a receptive heart, made-up mind, feet that are

fixed, firm and unmovable in the lord , that are not afraid
to let hell know "this means war"! They are dead serious
about repossessing all that the enemy has stolen.
Discerned or seeking discernment, fully armed, worded
up. These types of believers will make their mark and will
be able to endure to the end.

This race is not given to the quick nor the swift but
unto him who is able endure to the end. Sadly, the non-
believer who engulfs him/herself in ignorance, carnal
distractions, and the cares of this world will be deceived
and unfortunately, eventually devoured.

Recall if you will all the infamous cults that effectively
rose up through the 70's to early 90's. Cultism was an
entire vibe operating in "Plain Sight". Cult leader and
false prophet Jim Jones founded the "Peoples Temple"
in the 1950's. He deported roughly 900 people to
Jamestown, a makeshift village in Guyana where he
convinced his congregation of 900 people, of which, 276
were innocent children, to commit suicide by drinking
cool-aid laced with cyanide. If you would also recall the
Manson Family, established and developed by world
renowned cult leader , Charles Manson, a proud false
teacher, and crackhead. Duping his 100 cult followers
into blindly believing he was Jesus Christ, he gave his
revelation of false prophecy informing of an imminent,
apocalyptic "race war" looming in the immediate future.
In 1969, family members Susan Atkins, Tex Watson, and
Patricia Krenwinkel entered the home of Hollywood
actress Sharon Tate and murdered her and four other

innocent individuals minding their own business at her home. This was tragically carried out at his "sick sadist" command. Lastly, we have Credonia Mwerinde of Uganda. She was a high priestess, witch doctor and prostitute. She co- founded the "Movement for the Restoration of the Ten Commandments of God" in 1952. Her sect was a spin down of "Roman Catholic Witchcraft", devoting their lives and souls to the Virgin Mary also known as the "Queen of Heaven". Credonia linked up with False Prophet Joseph Kibweteere in 1989, telling him that the dead (laying in her grave) Virgin Mary advised her that he should give her a place to stay, shortly after they mutually agreed to be partners in sadism. Their evil mission gained great momentum growing expeditiously, estimating as many as 5,000 excommunicated catholic priests and nuns to run their satanic mission. When the world didn't end in year 2000 for "Y2K" like they said it would, there was an uprising of certain "awoke members" who then began to question these hypocrisies demanding a return on their investments. Both Credonia Mwerinde and Joseph Kibweteere swiftly took matters into their own hands to resolve the issue by locking 530 protestors inside the church and later burning them all alive while the two of them escaped safety. It is rumored that both are alive and chilling today. Sadly to say, people perish for lack of knowledge. In today's societal atmospheres, these types of cult- like assemblies are more irrelevant due to factors like inflation, management cost and more readily available using new age technology along with the ability for people to self-investigate people and organizations many are less likely to be pulled into these types of occult sects. That doesn't mean the tool of deception itself is any less relevant or prevalent. It simply means it is being redirected in a different form of facets. We still have to be on guard, be prayed up, sober, diligent and alert always. Nowadays many cult/sect leaders recruit on social media using

Facebook, Instagram and TikTok along with other various social media outlets as their sole vehicles of operation. Oftentimes, they seek out, misguided, naïve, uneducated, lonely people who accept their lies at face value. Other times the place of worship is perfectly poised as a legitimate place of worship but in all actuality is not. On my twenty-two year journey seeking Christ, I too have occasionally wandered into organizations that I later found out were nothing more than "glorified religious cults" "fronting in the Name of Jesus". Fortunately, it was never anything too detrimentally extreme and I was able to exit just as quickly as I entered, not being duped or brainwashed. For what we don't know can kill us. Ignorance of God's word is the enemies' ultimate weapon of defense. **Hosea 4:6** *"My people are destroyed for lack of knowledge, because you have rejected knowledge,"* I reiterate only spirit filled believers, that are worded- up, biblically, armed with the word, and fully dressed in the full armor of God will be able to defeat the Wiles of the devil and his demonic fiery darts. Only they will be able to firmly take a stand against the devils' scams, to overcome evil by doing good.

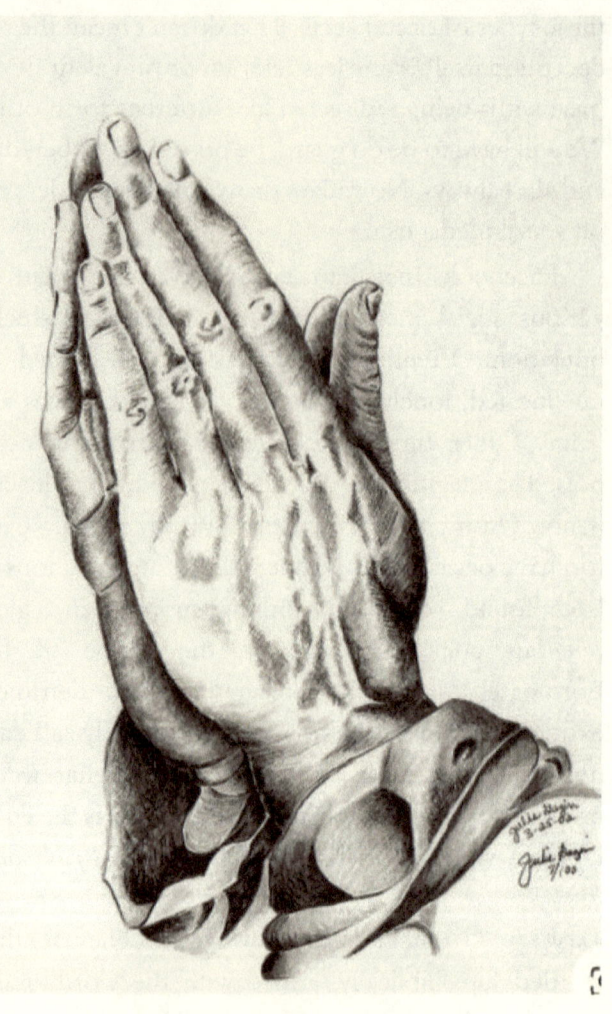

DISCERNMENT
OF HOLY SPIRIT

What is discernment? In the most minute term, discernment, as it relates to Christian spirituality may be defined as "Spiritual wisdom designated only from God. It cannot be bought, taught or replicated in any worldly higher institution of learning or church".

Acts 1:8 says *"But you will receive power when the Holy Spirit comes on you; and you will be my witnesses in Jerusalem, and in all Judea and Samaria, and to the ends of the earth."* Let us think back to Donald Lawrences' song "Spiritual" when he cited, "You're not a natural being Having a spiritual experience, but you're a spiritual being living this natural experience. When the fact that we are "Spiritual Beings" becomes clouded by the noise, distractions and the cares of this world we find ourselves at a crossroad that opens a door, either a door to understanding or a door to confusion. It's not unreasonable for a person's sole reason and purpose for existing seems to becomes distorted and at times almost completely voided, leaving that person susceptible and highly vulnerable to worldly carnal deception. An open target of being deceived gives the enemy a foothold.

Demons themselves are spiritual forces who are invisible to the natural eye but can be identified through their presence by discernment of the Holy Spirit. Because they are emotionless, reckless, futile, spiritual forces, they don't feel anything except for joy when they have caused an individual (especially a believer) to fall and slip out of God's will. It is vital to realize they cannot feel. Without discernment they cannot be seen or sensed, some while fully operating, full time, in a person's mind or in their heart on an ongoing basis. This is not a fight that can be won by emotions, violence, intelligence or man's hands. This is a spiritual war and must be fought in the spirit realm if a person is to receive their deliverance to overcome the chain that has them bound to witchcraft, brainwashing or spiritual manipulation. To be clear, punching a demon in the face will only render pointless and will quickly exhaust the flesh. Demons have forfeited their immortal souls, sentenced to an eternal hell, and have no emotions, nor do they have the ability to feel. Be mindful that most demons are persistent, clever and relentless in their pursuit of your soul, being physically qualified is also an important attribute and viable component to "Warring in The Spirit" against the kingdom of darkness, some stubborn generational demons can only be driven out by "fervent prayer" and "fasting". **2 Corinthians 10 3** *"For though we walk in the*

*flesh, we do not war after the flesh: For the weapons of our warfare
are not carnal, but mighty through God to the pulling down of strong
holds; Casting down imaginations, and every high thing that exalts
itself against the knowledge of God, and bringing into captivity every
thought to the obedience of Christ;"*

The standard dictionary defines discernment as, "the
quality of being able to grasp and comprehend what is
obscure; skill in discerning; an act of perceiving or
discerning something. Much the same applies to the
citizens of the kingdom of God, the covenant believer.
Discernment is a precious spiritual gift bestowed by the
Holy Spirit, which openly, outwardly or inwardly allows
an individual to distinguish and identify demonic or
heavenly influential spirits within or over a person, place,
or event.

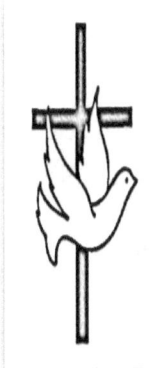

"Keep them and do them, for that will
be your wisdom and your understanding
in the sight of the peoples, who, when
they hear all these statutes, will say,
'Surely this great nation is a wise and
understanding people."
Deuteronomy 4:6

Isaiah 11:2 *"The Spirit of the LORD will rest on him—
the Spirit of wisdom and of understanding, the Spirit of counsel and
of might, the Spirit of the knowledge and fear of the LORD."*
When the Holy Spirit falls upon a person, believer or

nonbeliever, they shall receive power. Remember Saul before he became the Apostle Paul did not believe and was a persecutor of Christ and his followers. Consequently, through the miraculous gift of discernment that was bestowed upon him after he lost his sight, he became one of the most prevalent apostles responsible for contributing most books of the Bible.

The journey to overcoming entrapment to the devil's snare won't be an easy one but it will be one of the most fulfilling things you will have ever accomplished, if you stay faithful, don't lose heart and never give in. You will not regret the race you ran for your soul, with steadfast endurance. You will never regret the fact you ran it to win it possessing an outright refusal to be deceived by the world ruler of wickedness and deceit.

Philippians 1:9-10 - "And it is my prayer that your love may abound more and more, with knowledge and all discernment, so that you may approve what is excellent, and so be pure and blameless for the day of Christ."

Many will ask how can one seek after this powerful kingdom gift of "discernment". There are many ways to chase after, seek to acquire it, but the main one is by studying to show thyself approved. Study, study, study, get the word in you by any means necessary. Be committed to learning at least 7 warfare scriptures and committing them to memory that you will have written on your heart. Having them stored up for times when you may have to speak to those unseen things of satans kingdom. Be committed to establishing a relationship with God so when the deceiver comes. You will be filled with so much Holy Boldness that you will be able to look that demon in the face without fear, or fright and declare to the imp "You can't tell me nothing I know God for myself" Decree over yourself that "I will never be misled by man crafted philosophy and empty deception, according to the traditional and generational curses". By declaring to the enemy that you are not naïve to the Will of God or without understanding and you suffer no identity crises in the Lord. You then are already ten steps ahead of the game."

Hebrews 5:14 - "But solid food is for the mature, for those who have their powers of discernment trained by constant practice to distinguish good from evil."

Four ways to seek after and acquire discernment

1. Earnest Prayer

2. The Word of God

3. Instruction of the Holy Spirit

4. Hesitantly: I note "Wise Counsel"

Desiring true discernment always starts with open, honest heartfelt prayer or even a conversation with the only wise God, Jehovah, then sealed in the name of the "Promised Messiah Jesus Christ". God is a rewarder to those who diligently seek him. **Hebrews 11:6.** Secondly it is vital to be and stay " worded up". The word of God is the believer's unmistakable road map AKA Spiritual GPS, through this life's journey. The reason why so many believers are being deceived by our enemy, the devil, is because the devil is able to see and use their spiritual immaturity and ignorance of God's word . Brazenly he uses it against them. In the kingdom, ignorance is not bliss. **Hosea 4:6** states *"My people are destroyed for lack of knowledge. Because you have rejected knowledge, I also will reject you from being priest for me; Because you have forgotten the law of your God, I also will forget your children"*. As citizens of the Kingdom of God, there is an "eternal inheritance" on our lives that the devil can and will steal if we allow ourselves to be absent of God's word and commandments in which we are ordered to live. The heavens rejoice when believers and babes in Christ old and new seek and return home to him through his Holy Word. The most viable way is to heed instruction from the Holy Spirit, giving way to discernment. Discernment will never fail you. Even if you are a baby in Christ and feel as if you can't or don't hear from the Holy Spirit, don't fret and revert back to step one and two. God speaks to people and believers in many different versatile ways, not solely by direct speaking. It's up to us the believer to seek his face and heed his instruction, rather it comes directly from seeing, hearing the Word itself or a passage in scripture etc. This is a spiritual journey and one has to be willing to be led by the Spirit. The "Spirit of Truth" for God is a Spirit and who serves him, has to serve in "Spirit and Truth". Lastly and hesitantly: I note "Wise Counsil. Step four" can be a tricky roadway to deception; therefore, I advise approaching this step with caution and indecision. There is plenty of room to be deceived or digest inappropriate un wise counsel, often derived from lewd, human-crafted, false prophecy, if one is not, prayed up, worded up, armored up and able to discern and identify in the Spirit of God. Most cohorts from the devil, Possessed False Prophets or False Teachers are "dangerously intelligent" and highly astute in taking scripture and either polluting it with trivial insignificant theologies, twisting it to edify a "Worldly Carnal (sometimes satanic) Agenda." The word itself commands that we taste the fruit before we eat it. Therefor you have to assert and make sure the person rendering the counsel is really for God and from God! We are not commanded to naively accept the duplicity that the enemy is trying to force down our throats, for the consequences can be eternally deadly. The Bible lists at least 59 or more scriptures on deception see

1. **Matthew 24:4** "And Jesus answered and said to them, ' See to it that no one misleads you.'"

2. **Jeremiah 9:6**"Your dwelling is in the midst of deceit; Through deceit they refuse to know Me," declares the Lord.

3. **Romans 16:18** For such men are slaves, not of our Lord Christ but of their own appetites; and by their smooth and flattering speech they deceive the hearts of the unsuspecting.

4. **Matthew 24:11** Many false prophets will arise and will mislead many.

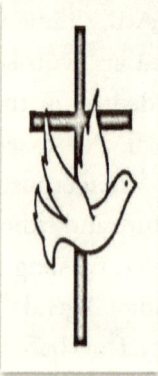

See to it that no one takes you captive through philosophy and empty deception, according to the tradition of men, according to the elementary principles of the world, rather than according to Christ.
Colossians 2:8

The Walk with God
is a Spiritual One!

This walk that we're on is a Spiritual Walk, the believer must do whatever he/she has to do in order to guard their heart, mind, spirit and soul from the wiles of the devil. The most efficient way is to soundly take a stand against the devil's scams, utilizing the word of God, prayer & fasting, as loaded armed securities when waging this warfare through discernment, we will not be deceived by flattering false speech or unpure words that are sweet like honey. **1 Timothy 4:1** *"But the Spirit explicitly says that in later times some will fall away from the faith, paying attention to deceitful spirits and doctrines of demons."*

Time is of the essence and no man knows the time nor the hour of Christ return, until that time comes, we must know that our enemy the devil roams around like a roaring lion seeking whom he may devour. **James 4 4** "Friendship with the world is enmity with God." We have to choose this day whom we are going to serve! Witchcraft and ungodly devices of destruction are being used daily by devout followers of the devil, flamboyantly they are being practiced every day, everywhere in plain sight. Every day, someone else is being spiritually defrauded and manipulated into eternal secret oaths or other types of carnal buffoonery, hailing homage to lucifer secretly and rendering ungodly allegiances to the devil not even being, aware.

Timothy 3 9

"But know this, that in the last days perilous times will come: For men will be lovers of themselves, lovers of money, boasters, proud, blasphemers, disobedient to parents, unthankful, unholy, unloving, unforgiving, slanderers, without self-control, brutal, despisers of good, traitors, headstrong, haughty, **lovers of pleasure rather than lovers of God***, having a form of godliness but denying its power. And from such people turn away! 6 For of this sort are those who creep into households and make captives of gullible women loaded down with sins, led away by various lusts, always* _learning and never able to come to the knowledge of the truth"_.

It's important to be diligently awoke, quick to listen and even quicker to ask appropriate biblical questions at the right time so that you are not deceived. Asking the right question and knowing the biblical answer can spare you an eternity of regret. The absurdity of modern-day False Prophecy is at an all-time high and the "Prosperity Fairy-Tale" is the fish bait ready to reel the unsuspecting in. Far too many people mistake the devil's evil, for his being stupid. He is in no way unintelligent and can sniff out the ones yearning for God. Consequently, he is also able to sense when a person's faith outweighs their willingness to work for it. Putting forth the necessary work to get the job done. Faith without works is dead. Studying, developing your own personal relationship with the Father which art in Heaven is key, then making sure your works parallel your faith at 50/50 ratio, neither being greater than the other. Sadly, it's with much consequence, that I must note the Lord will never anoint a listless or lazy individual that he can not count on. That is a religious pipe dream sold to keep worshipers pacified and subdued assured that they are never reaching for or acquiring their fullest potential. Faith without works is still dead, sleeping soundly in its grave.

See **1Corinthians 15:58** "Therefore, my beloved brothers, be steadfast, immovable, always abounding in the "work" of the Lord, knowing that in the Lord your labor is not in vain." While you are seeking true discernment, be relentless in your pursuit of God's Word, don't be conformed to this world but constantly be evolving your mind to the mind of Christ. Repositioning a learning mindset will be the most challenging part of the conquest to overcome these spiritual impediments, especially when carnality is always at war with spirituality, fear paralyzes faith. **1 Corinthians 2:14** "The *person without the Spirit does not accept the things that come from the Spirit of God but considers them foolishness, and cannot understand them because they are discerned only through the Spirit.*"

The kingdom of darkness AKA the satanic world of lucifer is in no way sluggish or stagnant in its evil pursuit to have us slip out of the will of God but is in fact very lively and active causing havoc, distress confusion, illnesses and unprecedented and unmerited evil and violence in this world. What he has prepared for everyday people as well as the believer will blindside many who are in no way prepared for the consequence. Common examples of spiritual manipulation are...

➢ Strict authoritarian cult-like control or behavior

➢ Lying and manipulating for a purpose that does not pertain to God's will, plans or purposes

➢ Selling or leasing spiritual gifts, including but not limited to , the anointing, so called healing handkerchiefs, Holy Water from the faucet etc.

➢ Being excessively money hungry / thirsty to the point of theft or embezzlement or exploitation of the vulnerable children & families, children and of the elderly

➢ Using authorities and power to extort or receive sexual favors

➢ Sexual perversion and abuse. Using titles to cover up the gross act of sexual abuse or exploitation, especially in the church

➢ The misuse or no use of Jesus' name within a congregation

Just to name a few, there are no golden VIP tickets to heaven. Speaking of which, an example of this unacceptable behavior, according to egypttoday.com a Cairo Pastor Tito Watts, a Zimbabwe based clergyman, and his wife, Amanda, were arrested for selling "tickets to heaven." According to the police, the Pastor and his wife scammed people into buying $500 tickets that should have gotten them into the gates of heaven, with no judgment. What's sadder than that, was that more than likely; these were poor people and families already struggling to get by, living paycheck to paycheck, scraping up their last to be squandered on a pipe dream. The devil saw both their desire for God but also their absence of wisdom and knowledge of God's Word, therefore leaving them wide open for deception they were able to be deceived. In Brooklyn, a self-proclaimed pastor known as the "Bling Bishop of Brooklyn" stole the identities of at least hundreds of people which he hacked from his then girlfriend's computer. He took out loans in their names and bought cars and motorcycles, jewelry and expensive clothes, and properties according to his indictment and arrest report in Suffolk County in 2006. The Bling Bishop alleged that during the five-year prison term, he found God and was ready to turn his life around. The fact is, he really spent those five years conjuring up the perfect scam and scheme of the devil, while doing time in federal prison. Five years later he opened and branded a so-called church where he continued on his defraud-ing and brainwashing mission of naive church members until he was arrested and arraigned on fraud charges. These incidents are not solely based in the Church alone, they are becoming more prevalent in today's society. The invisible war has never been livelier than it is now. The word of God warns us to be sober, be diligent and alert, for our prevalent adversary the devil roams around like a roaring lion seeking whom he may devour. **1 Peter 5:8.** If we are blindsided or ignorant to God's Word, we leave ourselves -open to this vulnerability. His biggest weapons of offense are

1. **Ignorance of God's Word**
2. **Conformity and Naivety**
3. **Rebellion against God's law.**
4. **Lukewarmness serving two masters.**

Demons adversely influence the choices, behavior, and speech of those of whom they take over and possess. Once an evil spirit has taken full possession of the being, the flesh has little to no control going forth. Common signs that demons or demonic influence or demonic possession are behind your choices is when you either radically hate or irrationally love the choices you make yet you keep making the same choices with little to no self-control. **Romans 6:1-7** *"What should we say then? Should we continue to sin so that God's kindness_will increase? That's unthinkable! As far as sin is concerned, we have died. So how can we still live under sin's influence? God Forbid."*

Demons adversely affect the state of mind engulfing the individual's mind with thoughts of destruction, hate, and mischievous evil. Without intervention. Intercession or deliverance the state of the individual's being possessed, the demonic interference or possession will significantly worsen. (See Luke 11:23-26) Demons can discern the presence of God's anointing, his anointed, holiness and the holy spirit, prophets, true prayer warriors. In their relentless pursuit to honor their unholy contractual commitment to Lucifer they audaciously rebel, wreaking havoc, discord and division. They react with hostile paranoia, anger and resentment, envy, phoniness, rage, and vile accusations (See Mark 5:1-20) Especially fleshly decisions, character assassinations, accusations and worldly judgments. The first hint of a demonic influence or position is to emphatically know and understand that, only a devil, is the accuser of thy brethren, constantly imputing confusion, division and dysfunctional discords.

Ecclesiastes 8:5 He who keeps his command will experience nothing harmful; And a wise man's heart discerns both time and judgment

Ephesians 4 17-18 This I say, therefore, and testify in the Lord, that you should no longer walk as the rest of the Gentiles walk, in the futility of their mind, having their understanding darkened, being alienated from the life of God, because of the ignorance that is in them, because of the blindness of their heart;

John 3:16

DISCERNING
WITCHCRAFT

Witchcraft is a committed, dedicated evil between one person with the devil to carry out evil acts of wickedness introvertedly and outwardly toward another person, groups, places or organizations. Witchcraft uses spiritual evil powers, rituals, spells, astute brainwashing techniques to recruit, subdue, control, manipulate and cause harm to others by way of divination, ouija-boards, false religions, false prophecy, spiritual manipulation, brain washing, white magic, black magic, sorcery, rituals, spell casting, chaotic missions that cause havoc, division and destruction. Including but not limited to evil assignments, cultic religions, secret societies, sorcery, perversion, idolatry, tarot reading, idol worship, bowing down to or vowing oaths to false idol gods, false prophets or evil altars and communication with the dead.

2 Chronicles 33:6 "He sacrificed his children in the fire in the Valley of Ben Hinnom, practiced divination and witchcraft, sought omens, and consulted mediums and spiritists. He did much evil in the eyes of the Lord, arousing his anger."

10 "There shall not be found among you anyone who makes his son or his daughter pass through the fire, or one who practices witchcraft, or a soothsayer, or one who interprets omens, or a sorcerer,"
Deuteronomy 18:10

Micah 5:12 "I will destroy your witchcraft and you will no longer cast spells."

Nahum 3:4 "all because of the wanton lust of a prostitute, alluring, the mistress of sorceries, who enslaved nations by her prostitution and peoples by her witchcraft."

Galatians 5:20 "idolatry and witchcraft; hatred, discord, jealousy, fits of rage, selfish ambition, dissensions, factions"

In Valerie Love "13 Signs you're a Witch" she boastfully identifies the various types of Witch you should be on guard against.

➤ Kitchen Witch
➤ Christian Witch
➤ Catholic Witch
➤ Pagan Witch
➤ Evangelical Witch
➤ Music Witch

The Kitchen Witch personifies the reason why you cannot afford to eat every one's cooking. Nor can you afford to eat from everyone's dwelling place if you truly don't know them on a personal level. Valerie Love tells you *"Her kitchen was the sanctuary and temple from which she worked her Magick, creating delicacies no one could replicate."* **The Christian Witch** is why you cannot believe everyone you meet in the Church is always necessarily a Christian. Valerie Love the proud self-proclaimed witch goes on to say "a *Witch who integrates Christ and the Craft in their Magickal and spiritual practices. A Christian Witch may employ Bible Magick, Angel Magick, Bibliomancy (Bible divination) and Psalms blessings and hexings."* The Next is the **Catholic Witch** this is why we reject False Teachers, prophets and idol worship. *Valerie Love reiterates that "there are a whole host of Catholic Witches in our global community. Catholicism has its fair share of Magick, so it's not surprising that adherents to the faith would consciously choose to seek a deeper and more personally meaningful space where Magick and the Catholic Church converge.*

These witches didn't turn their back on what they hold as beautiful in the Catholic Church because they decided to honor their inner Witch. Instead, they integrated the energies into a harmonic whole that pleases the soul." Another is the **Pagan Witch.** *Why you should most definitely arm yourself against thriving Pagan Traditions in American Culture. She clarifies its alias as being the Christo-Pagan Witch. Valerie Love defines them as "The ChristoPagans I know who are Witches have discovered and/or created stunningly beautiful ways to integrate Paganism (Earth Based Religion) with the mystical life and teachings of Christ. We can't forget the* **Music Witch AKA Witch As An ARTIST.** Valerie Love mentions Beyonce 15 times in her publication insinuating her art boldly and outright reflects modern day pagan witchcraft, this is what she says, "Beyonce is a Witch artist if ever I've seen one. By her artistic and at times enigmatic self-admission, she is a daughter of Oshun. While I've never heard her say that in words, I've seen her convey the message with her art." *Lastly, she illustrates the* **Evangelical Witch.** *"Yes, I know one. She can preach a sermon like you wouldn't believe, and her Witchy room is off the charts.* Many false teachers, false prophets and fake pastors have gone out in the world and mostly all are on the devil's payroll . A tree is known by its fruits and the fruits by its tree. Don't be so quick to be convinced that everyone who preaches a good sounding sermon, professes with their mouth they are a Christian actually are. It is written that many will praise God with their mouths but their hearts are far from HIM.

Now at this point being appalled, hopefully you haven't gagged at unactual audacity which insinuates that Christianity *could ever actually be combined with the pagan practice of Witchcraft and still be viewed as honorable by God is obscured and absurd.*

"Do not turn to mediums or seek out spiritists, for you will be defiled by them. I am the LORD your God"
Leviticus 19:31

Chronicles 33:6 "He sacrificed his children in the fire in the Valley of Ben Hinnom, practiced divination and witchcraft, sought omens, and consulted mediums and spiritists. He did much evil in the eyes of the LORD, arousing his anger."

Both Saul & Jezebel used witchcraft to get what they wanted and later died harsh and peculiar deaths as a result. The occult was created and branded to specifically execute "Extra- Ordinary Mind Control" by any means necessary even unto the selling of one's soul. The NKJV Woman's Study Bible defines Occultism as "intimately involving various types of demonic secret techniques directed at altering human consciousness, peering into and manipulating the supernatural in order to attain psycho-spiritual powers."

Occultic Witchcraft Practices include but are not limited to.

➢ Spiritism: making contact with deceased or invisible personalities through spirit mediums or through trance channeling or a form of voluntary possession (1 Samuel 28 3-30)

➢ Fortune Telling: using a wide variety of methods and objects to give advice (Acts 16 16-18

➢ Astrology: the ancient method of mapping celestial events by means of horoscopes (Is 47 13-15 San 2:2, 5-7

➢ Numerology: which attracts special significance to numbers and uses those numbers to analyze character and to predict the future. (Gen 41 1-3)

➢ Palmistry: which interprets the future by analyzing the lines on the palms of the hands

➢ Tarot Cards: which uses the special occultic symbols to predict the future

➢ Aut"omic Writing: in which the participant writes in a trance like state without conscious control.

These are various ways witchcraft can be utilized.

1. **False Religions**
2. **New Age Religions**
3. **Hypnotism**
4. **Yoga (Om Chants)**
5. **Ungodly Associations**
6. **Pornography**
7. **Educational Institutions**
8. **Sororities**
9. **Secret Societies**
10. **False Church**
11. **False Religions**
12. **Idolatries**
13. **False Religions**
14. **Sorcery**
15. **Divination**
16. **Bullying & Intimidation**
17. **Tarot Reading**
18. **Covenants & Contracts**
19. **Brain-Washing**
20. **Manipulation**
21. **Intimidation**
22. **Inflict Harm**
23. **Intimidation**
24. **Control**
25. **Spiritual Exploitation**
26. **Rituals**
27. **Spiritual intimidation**

28. **Casting Spells**
29. **Imitating & Hating God**
30. **TV/Movies**
31. **Peeking into secret things**
32. **Music Hip Hop/Heavy Metal**
33. **Attack God's People & the Church**

All of these are Co practices Belial and are demonic in origin and prohibited by scripture **(Deut. 18: 10,11)** Entertaining satanic occult practices and Witchcraft of any sort opens a door and possibly a portal to many demons which paves the way to Emotional Bondage and Spiritual Slavery, Mental illness, suicide, insomnia, destruction, sickness, addiction and perversion, sadism, lust etc.

Deuteronomy 18:10-14 " Let no one be found among you who sacrifices their son or daughter in the fire, who practices divination or sorcery, interprets omens, engages in witchcraft, or casts spells, or who is a medium or spiritist or who consults the dead. Anyone who does these things is detestable to the LORD; because of these same detestable practices the LORD, your God will drive out those nations before you."

1 Samuel 15:23

SATAN'S KINGDOM VS KINGDOM OF GOD

Let's be clear there are two kingdoms, God's Kingdom and satans Kingdom. Both very real, both serving two distinctly different purposes. There's God's kingdom, the Kingdom of Heaven and there's satan's kingdom the Kingdom of Darkness. In order to get a better grasp on not being deceived it's important to declaratively know what God you are serving and what Kingdom he is ruling. It is also imperative to recognize where God has brought you from especially if you profess to have been saved and born again.

Any man that be in Christ Jesus is a new creation **2 Corinthians 5:17** There is a distinguishing difference between God's Kingdom and satan's Kingdom. Growing Deep and Strong Ministries describe *the difference as, "There is a radical difference between the Kingdom of Darkness and the Kingdom of Light. The nature of the Kingdom of Darkness is an eternity of spiritual slavery and leads to eternal death—separation* *from God and from everyone else; but the nature of the Kingdom of Light is eternal life.*"

We will touch on the

7 Legal Rights to Citizens of The Kingdom

1. The right to be Free

Galatians 5:1: "For freedom Christ has set us free; stand firm therefore, and do not submit again to a yoke of slavery"

2. The Right to be Healed

Isaiah 53:5 " But He was wounded for our transgressions, He was bruised for our iniquities; The chastisement for our peace was upon Him, And by His stripes we are healed.

3. The Right to Repentance

Romans 3 20-24

Therefore, by the deeds of the law there shall no flesh be justified in his sight: for by the law is the knowledge of sin. But now the righteousness of God without the law is manifested, being witnessed by the law and the prophets; *Even the righteousness of God which is by faith of Jesus Christ unto all and upon all them that believe: for there is no difference: For all have sinned, and come short of the glory of God; Being justified freely by his grace through the redemption that is in Christ Jesus:*

4. **The Right to live a Fearless Life**

   Isaiah 41:10 "Fear not, for I am with you; be not dismayed, for I am your God; I will strengthen you, I will help you, I will uphold you with my righteous right hand"

5. **The Right to Live in Peace**

   Philippians 4:7 And the peace of God, which surpasses all understanding, will guard your hearts and your minds in Christ Jesus. **John 14 -27** "Peace I leave with you, My peace I give to you; not as the world gives do I give to you. Let not your heart be troubled, neither let it be afraid."

6. **Right to Triumph**

   2 Corinthians 2:14 Now thanks be unto God, which always causeth us to triumph in Christ, and maketh manifest the savior of his knowledge by us in every place.

7. Right to Kingdom Armor, Christ Blood, The Word of God, Jesus Name, Fervent Prayer, and The Holy Spirit

Ephesians 6-10 Finally, my brethren, be strong in the Lord, and in the power of his might. Put on the whole armor of God, that ye may be able to stand against the wiles of the devil. For we wrestle not against flesh and blood, but against principalities, against powers, against the rulers of the darkness of this world, against spiritual wickedness in high places. Wherefore take unto you the whole armor of God, that ye may be able to withstand in the evil day, and having done all, to stand. Stand therefore, having your loins girt about with truth, and having on the breastplate of righteousness; And your feet shod with the preparation of the gospel of peace; Above all, taking the shield of faith, wherewith ye shall be able to quench all the fiery darts of the wicked one. And take the helmet of salvation, and the sword of the Spirit, which is the word of God: Praying always with all prayer and supplication in the Spirit, and watching thereunto with all perseverance and supplication for all saints; And for me, that utterance may be given unto me, that I may open my mouth boldly, to make known the mystery of the gospel,

The greatest affliction among Believers and Unbelievers alike is identity crisis in the Kingdom of God. Suffering an identity crisis in the Lord is like, having a vested billion-dollar insurance policy you never knew anything about. Except instead of insurance, we have a Blessed Assurance, which is God's Covenant to all who have full faith,

believe, and confess Jesus Christ as Lord, repents and keeps God's commandments. Part of that earthly benefit is obtaining a legal authoritative right as a child of God.

Matthew 5:3 ESV "Blessed are the poor in spirit, for theirs is the kingdom of heaven."

Matthew 5:10 *"Blessed are those who are persecuted for righteousness' sake, for theirs is the kingdom of heaven*

Gods Kingdom	Satans Kingdom
Kingdom of Light	Kingdom of Darkness
Joy, Rejoicing, Many Mansions, infinite beauty	Torment, Horror, Torture to the gnashing of teeth
7 Spirits of God who sit before his throne	Lucifer, The Beast, The False Prophet & the Antichrist
God Head & Holy Trinity	Unholy Trinity
Angelic Hierarchy	Regimented Forces Hierarchy
Angels	Fallen Angels/Demons
Weapons, Praise, Word of God and Faith, Full Armor, Blood of Christ and the power of his name,	Witchcraft, Ignorance, Brainwashing, Spiritual Manipulation, Soul Wounds, Deception, Depression, Anger
Gift/ Reward Salvation	Cost of sin is death

Mark 9:1 "And he said to them, 'Truly, I say to you, there are some standing here who will not taste death until they see the kingdom of God after it has come with power.'"

 "Then the seventh angel blew his trumpet, and there were loud voices in heaven, saying, "The kingdom of the world has become the kingdom of our Lord and of his Christ, and he shall reign forever and ever."

Revelation 11:15

Daniel 2:44 "And in the days of those kings the God of heaven will set up a kingdom that shall never be destroyed, nor shall the kingdom be left to another people. It shall break in pieces all these kingdoms and bring them to an end, and it shall stand forever."

Matthew 11:12 "From the days of John the Baptist until now the kingdom of heaven has suffered violence, and the violent take it by force."

EVIL ALTARS & YOKES

Defining, what exactly an altar is? An altar is a structure in which offerings are made to God, a deity or foreign Gods. Altars could be natural objects or man-made constructs (i.e., dresser, stand, stage or pulpit. Stone altars are structures of earth **Exodus 20:24** or unwrought stone, on which sacrifices were offered. The word altar as it pertains to scripture is cited in **Hebrew 13:10** for the sacrifice offered upon it, the sacrifice Christ offered. "The Apostle Paul found among the many altars erected in Athens one bearing "the inscription, "To the unknown God **Exodus 20:24.** An altar of earth you shall make for me and sacrifice on it your burnt offerings and your peace offerings, your sheep and your oxen. In every place where I cause my name to be remembered, I will come to you and bless you."

It is crucially imperative to understand what an altar is and its sole purpose. What it has been used for in times past and what it will be used for in this present time. As mentioned in the previous chapter "Discerning Witchcraft". We discussed the various types of modern-day Pagan

Witches operating in every day functions of society. Therefore, for the sake of this conversation we will focus on <u>The Stage</u>, <u>The Table</u> and <u>The Pulpit</u>. We have already established the fact that an altar can be any structure in which sacrificial offerings can be offered to Yahweh or a deity (Idol God).

Hands down, the stage has been an open viable arena of worship for centuries, it can be a place to praise and worship God or it too can be a place to praise and worship the devil(Indirectly & indiscreetly).

Sadly, the stage can also be an open breeding ground for the "unsuspecting" especially if the believer is not cognizant of what they come in alignment with, agree with, praised or worshiped from that stage. Thats knowingly or unknowingly. What better place for unbelievers and devout followers of Lucifer to honor him in an all-out demonic sacrifice? Let's be clear, typical modern day Babylonian sacrifices would indeed be likely to include possessions like raging fire, blood, flesh (Human or Animal), Skulls and Skeletons, carved engraved images, satanic jewelry or costume mirroring lucifer, the bull, goat, snake or serpent, hot sex on a platter, statues poised as idol deity (e.g. goat, bull, snake,),666 symbols, demonic possession, death or reenactment of death, destruction, human sacrifice, white magic ,satanic magic tricks, black magic, hailing to or bowing down to glorified prostitutes or "jezebel prodigies" worshiping and giving homage to the whore of Babylon. Practical nakedness or scandalously clad dressing. Let us not leave out the infamous "all hail satan" devil salute. Just to name a few. You thought this was

Babylonian Circus, Bye! This is just another night at the Grammys (the same with the BET Awards). Every year the Grammys in what is supposed to be a mere musical award show honoring outstanding talent and achievements within the music industry over the years has systematically evolved into one of the most satanic, sacrificial altar call in world's history. The sad fact is that every year another soul is a target and possibly drafted into satans web of deceit. Hypnotically drawn to the TV and lured into the devils' evil web of deceit the evil show consistently draws in, clueless mothers, fathers, families, young children and teens. They will unknowingly go before the sacrifice being devoured, deceived and sometimes tricked into worshiping a false god or idols. Any form of hailing to or bowing down is a form of worship intentionally or unintentionally. This manner of evil altar call is, worldly, carnal, and holds the utmost disrespect to Yahweh above. See **Matthew 24:4** "And Jesus answered and said to them,'See to it that no one misleads you.'"

"Let no one deceive you with empty words, for because of these things the wrath of God comes upon the sons of disobedience. " *kingdom of our Lord and of his Christ, and he shall reign forever and ever.*"

Ephesians 5:6

2 Timothy 3:13 "But evil men and seducers shall wax worse and worse, deceiving, and being deceived." **1 Timothy 4:1** Now the Spirit speaketh expressly, that in the latter times some shall depart from the faith, giving heed to seducing spirits, and doctrines of devils; **2 Thessalonians 2:3** "Let no man deceive you by any means: for that day shall not come, except there come a falling away first, and that man of sin be revealed, the son of perdition;"

Next the table, this is where I highly caution woke people and believers alike about blindly picking, purchases and bringing used furniture into your home without having some type of prior knowledge about its past. It is alleged by the children of the parents who moved into Amityville Horror house that after the sadistic murders occurred, they for a period of time were brutally tormented in that demon-infested home because the parents were too cheap to invest into new furniture for the kids or the home. The children were made to sleep on the same beds the murders took place. That's right, they effortlessly looked as their children developed all types of mental and physiological problems from having been tormented and tortured by demons and evil paranormal occurrences day and night. These territorial demons had been sworn in and implemented to that region and the property refusing to leave. For instance, if you bring a table or dresser into your home that was once used for, satanic sacrifice, voodoo, hoodoo, santeria or any type of satanic sacrifice, it is a "cursed object" in the eyes of God. Such cursed things may very well bring a curse under your roof as well. Many have done so unconsciously, not understanding where these types of evil interference came about and was allowed in. Without the proper kingdom tools and resources many remain un unarmed and vulnerable to these types of spiritual attacks. Also, the same applies to the podium. Lastly we have the Pulpit, if the individual preaching from it is not truly a man or woman of God, it too may be the perfect vessel of an Evil Altar, where sacrifices are actually being given over to various demons and deities and not Jehovah the only true "Wise God". If it doesn't look right, smell right or taste right, don't swallow it. You wouldn't openly swallow and digest rotten food, so why then would willfully digest spoiled spiritual food that is condemnation to your soul?

Many occultic secret societies perform their evil sacrifices through leaders that are highly astute, adept resourceful and intelligent in not just knowing how, but extremely experienced in twisting the Word of God to "utter circumstantial confusion" it is often a bait and switch tactic to wheel you into their bait for the switch; benefiting satan's kingdom. The occultopedia describes a few modern-day secret societies as being, free masons, illuminati, klu klux klan, kappa alpha psi, beta sigma psi and Jehovah witnesses just to name a few. All require Oaths and Hellish rituals in order to become a member. Every one standing in a pulpit (even if they are holding a bible) is not necessarily a man or woman of God. The devil has held many Bibles in his hands and studied more often than most Bishops and to this day parades himself as an angel of light. Fruit has to be tested before eaten. Please don't be deceived.

An Evil Altar

It is a spiritual dining table where demons (devout worshipers and servants of satan) are called to eat, plot, gossip, assassinate characters and cause havoc among God's people. It's a place for one to block their own blessings. **2 Kings 3:15-19, 26-27.** Evil altars are worship hubs for evil spirits, followers of the occult, worshipers of satan, demons and principalities. It's a place where spells black/white magic is cast.

Evil Alters

"This is the sign that the LORD has spoken: 'Behold, the altar shall be torn down, and the ashes that are on it shall be poured out.'" And when the king heard the saying of the man of God, which he cried against the altar at Bethel, Jeroboam stretched out his hand from the altar, saying, "Seize him." And his hand, which he stretched out against him, dried up, so that he could not draw it back to himself. The altar also was torn down, and the ashes poured out from the altar, according

to the sign that the man of God had given by the word of the LORD"
1 Kings 13:11

It's a place where people are bewitched and spiritually manipulated to sin. **Numbers 25: 1-3,6-9, 31:15.**

It's a place where evil oaths are sworn, evil covenants are entered and perverse demonic rituals are performed... Essentially it is a place where people are spiritually arrested, blinded by the enemy satan and taken captive by the devil's regimented forces only to be released into life-long sentence of spiritual or mental slavery. **Acts 19: 23-25, 28-29, 32, 37-41**

Sacred Alters of God

An altar of earth you shall make for me and sacrifice on it your burnt offerings and your peace offerings, your sheep and your oxen. In every place where I cause my name to be remembered I will come to you and bless you.
Exodus 20:24

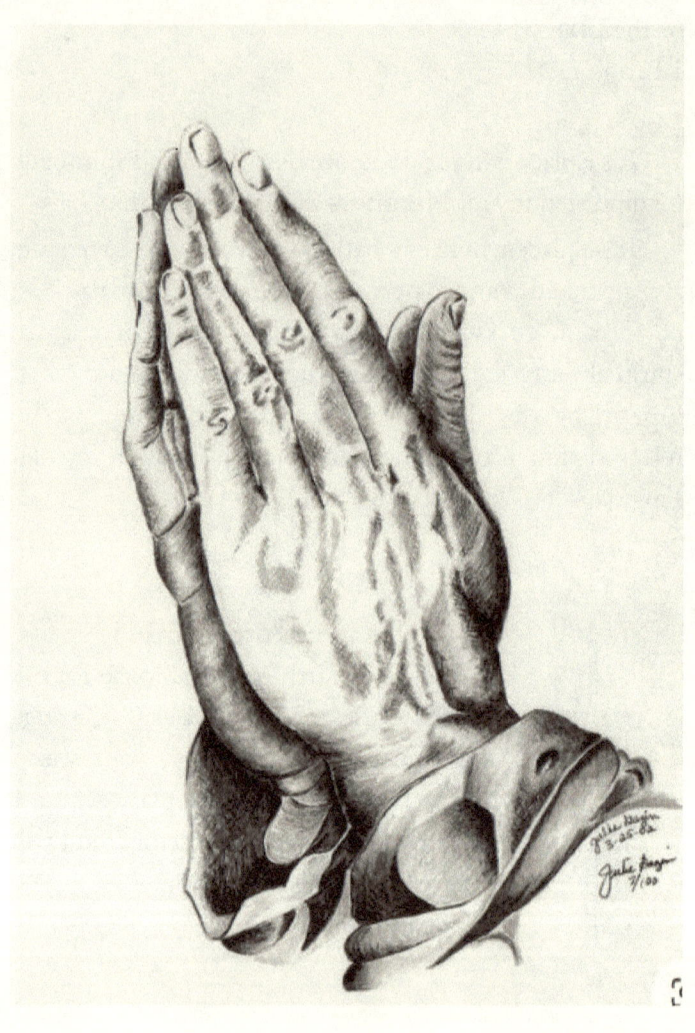

Genesis 9:9

COVENANTS CONTRACTS

2 Kings 23:3 Next, the king stood by the pillar and made a covenant in the presence of the Lord to follow the Lord and to keep His commands, His decrees, and His statutes with all his mind and with all his heart, and to carry out the words of this covenant that were written in this book; all the people agreed to the covenant.

A covenant is a devoted unwavering commitment between two parties or one party and a group. Typically involving or outlaying a life-or-death agreement or stipulation between two parties. It is an irrevocable legal agreement that will be honored and cannot be broken. The brokenness of the covenant can lead to curses or even death.

Deuteronomy 28 1-14 "If you indeed obey the LORD your God and are careful to observe all his commandments, I am giving you today, the LORD your God will elevate you above all the nations of the earth. [2] All these blessings will come to you in abundance if you obey the LORD your God: [3] You will be blessed in the city and blessed in the field[j] [4] Your children will be blessed, as well as the produce of your soil, the offspring of your livestock, the calves of your herds, and the lambs of your flocks. [5] Your basket and your mixing bowl will be blessed. [6] You will be blessed when you come in and blessed when you go out. [7] The LORD will cause your enemies who attack you to be struck down before you; they will attack you from one direction but flee from you in seven different directions. [8] The LORD will decree blessing for you with respect to your barns and in everything you do—yes, he will bless you in the land he is giving you. [9] The LORD will designate you as his holy people just as he promised you, if you keep his commandments and obey him.[k] [10] Then all the peoples of the earth will see that you belong to the LORD,[l] and they will respect you. [11] The LORD will greatly multiply your children, the offspring of your livestock, and the produce of your soil in the land that he promised your ancestors he would give you. [12] The LORD will open for you his good treasure house, the heavens, to give you rain for the land in its season and to bless all you do; you will lend to many nations but you will not borrow from any. [13] The LORD will make you the head and not the tail, and you will always end up at the top and not at the bottom, if you obey his commandments that I am urging you today to be careful to do. [14] But you must not turn away from all the commandments I am giving you today, to either the right or left, nor pursue other gods and worship them.

The curses for breaking covenant with God as described in Deuteronomy 28 is way far more stringent and severe than the blessings they are listed as.

> ➤ Curses as Reversal of Blessings
> ➤ Curses by Disease and Drought
> ➤ Curses by Defeat and Deportation
> ➤ The Curse of Military Siege
> ➤ The Curse of Covenant Termination

DISCERNING THE SPIRIT OF JEZEBEL

Jezebel, the evil queen, idol worshiper, madam, false prophetess, manipulator, prostitute, murderer and proud prosecutor of God's Prophets. It is important to recognize how prevalent her spirit is even in modern-day times today, especially adding to the desecration and decay of most modern-day churches. Yes, that is correct the same wiles of the devil (fornication, politics, division, greed, false prophecy, hate, envy, jealousy, murder: starting with-in the heart, drama, conformity, lukewarmness, chaos & confusion, weak leaders & even weaker pastors and hypocrites). Disastrously that's why we have so many empty, vanishing and perishing churches becoming even drastically more extinct day by day, even as we speak. Detrimentally; Pastors, Preachers and Bishops are preaching to the angels in empty sanctuaries while millions are perishing to the Wiles of the devil in the streets.

For the purpose of this literature, we will minutely explore who Jezebel was for the sake of educational purposes only. Towards the end of this publication, we will be proficient in binding up the Spirit of Jezebel & her Co-Witch Army. We Plead the Blood of Jesus on us and against them. We rebuke the spirit of manipulation and witchcraft. We stand in the gap and make intercession on behalf of those who can't. We bind the wicked spirit of Jezebel and loose the Army of God to unleash the Holy Spirit on Jezebel after the dog's finish devouring her flesh. **2 Kings 9:10.** Hopefully you will join me in snatching this heffa by her Lace Front Wig and casting her right back into fiery pits of hell where she belongs that every portal to Sheol is hereby closed and sealed.

The invisible war is very much real. This fight is not for the cowardly, weak, naive or feeble-minded . Once a person decides to pick up their cross and take a stand against the devils' scams to overcome and become "loosed" against the chains which once had them bound. They must be steadfast, firm fixed and unmovable ever abounding in and through the word of God.

We will focus primarily on Jezebel (aka Queen Witch) and the Babylonian Goddess "Mary" otherwise known as "Queen of Heaven". Both intricate forces of idol worship and occultic witchcraft.

Jezebel the daughter of Ithobaal , king of Tyre. Married King Ahab who ruled Israel at the time, promptly seducing and manipulating him into introducing the foreign idol worship of the Tyrian idol god of Baal (AKA Lucifer himself). Outright displaying a gross, vulgar desecration not only to God, but also to his commandments as well as his church. It wouldn't end

there, this was only the first of many vile acts to come
disregarding and disrespecting Yahweh the God of
Israel's law, commandments, heaven and earth. An evil
woman defiled with many wicked and perverse spirits,
possessing no moral compass or integrity was relentless
in getting what she wanted to further her evil mission to
destroy God's Church as well as his "TRUE" prophets.
A woman comprised of debased perverted energy. She
seductively manipulated weak obtuse mindless leaders
and clergymen of the church to overthrow God's
commandments to further her agenda of promoting the
idol god Baal(Idolatress Replica of Lucifer) over the true
God, Yahweh. Having hated God and hating his all-
powerful word, many of Yahweh's prophets were killed
and destroyed at her swift command. Jezebel the wicked
queen of Israel during the 9th century BC led the
covenant people into the worship of Pagan gods breaking
their commandments to God. She was audacious, a
strong-willed character who manipulated and controlled
others into doing exactly what she wanted in order to get
her way. The name Jezebel means without cohabitation.
Jezebel refused to live together or to cohabit with anyone
who refused to kiss her behind, she yielded to no
authority except her own, she couldn't be told anything.
She encouraged Yahweh's worshipers to commit both
spiritual and physical fornication by openly indulging in
idolatrous worship of hideous pagan gods and sex rituals
in the church. These disrespectful blasphemous acts were
unbearable and repulsive to Yahweh, he condemned

Jezebel, her husband and all of their offspring to death. In **Revelation 2 20** "The Church of Taitra is rebuked for passively allowing and tolerating the woman Jezebel to openly defile God's house of prayer overtly bringing in idol gods into the church for the people of Israel to worship. The original Jezebel had been dead for nearly 1000 years when another false prophetess with the same name somehow had appeared in the 1st century church , faking the funk and closely mimicking all of the evil intent and workings of the first Jezebel; she was fiercely independent, rebellious, controlling and unsubmissive and character and in action alike.

Jezebel led the people of God into idolatry and immorality under the counterfeit camouflage of religion while weak , scared, feeble mind minded leaders and clergymen looked on as if nothing was going on at all. She promoted and hyphened delusional claims that she was able to tap into the secret mysteries and the depths of God's knowledge bewitching most of the church as well as leaders to her persuasive dogmas. Sadly, she conjured up enough likeness to the principles of Yahweh's teachings that she was able to mislead, bewitch and seduce Christ's servants into being led away to serve foreign idol gods.

In essence her degenerate mysticism & incitements of witchcraft inevitably promoted and incited the spiritual wickedness of satan himself by coercing followers to accept and confess idolatry in a Pagan state of worship. Jezebel exemplifies a spirit of prideful independence and rebellion against God, his Prophets and his Church. Her treacherous spirit conceitedly directs Christians to a fleshly, carnal mindset of the world, it is a spirit that God does not tolerate and God will destroy.

"Behold, I send you out as sheep among the wolves. Therefore, be wise as serpents and harmless as doves
Matthew 10:16

Matthew 7:13-20 Wide *is* the gate and broad *is* the way that leads to destruction, and there are many who go in by it.

1. A Jezebel spirit is a female seductress.

2. A Jezebel spirit is a killer and prostitute. She murders first with a slanderous tongue. She uses her body and her physical attributes to obtain the things she lusts for.

3. Jezebel exploits and over step's her authority. Possesses a strong-willed rebellious passion for control.

4. A Jezebel spirit is manipulative and loves to conquer the weak and feeble men and women alike. She will play on your heart and emotions to achieve her evil desire, don't wear them on your sleeve.

5. A Jezebel spirit has a narcissistic personality. Never accepts guilt or responsibility, always very defensive

6. A Jezebel spirit is absent of a hard work ethic or morals, she uses beauty and sex to her advantage.

7. Jezebel serves Baal (AKA Lucifer).Baal was the god of prosperity, god of the harvests, god of fertility and sex. Calls herself a prophetess but is a false teacher and false prophetess.

8. A Jezebel spirit boasts about being a Prophetess but in reality, she is really a false Prophet lusting for and willfully catering to the wiles of the devil.

9. A Jezebel spirit will detest the true Gospel as the emphatical Word of God as well as his True Prophets.

10. A Jezebel spirit is a liar. She lies and has no problem bearing false witness. She is a gossiper with a slanderous/murderous tongue. She tears down more than she ever plans on building up. Edifying is never on her agenda.

Isaiah 42:8 (Amplified Bible)
I am the Lord; that is My name! And My glory I will not give to another, nor My praise to graven images.

Isaiah 47:5 (Amplified Bible)
"Sit in silence, go into darkness, Daughter of the Babylonians; no more will you be called queen of kingdoms

Queen of Heaven

Jeremiah 44:25 (Amplified Bible)"25 Thus says the Lord of hosts, the God of Israel: You and your wives have both declared with your mouths and fulfilled it with your hands, saying, we will surely perform our vows that we have vowed to burn incense to the queen of heaven and to pour out drink offerings to her. [Surely] then confirm your vows and [surely] perform your vows! [If you will defy all My warnings to you, then, by all means, go ahead!]"

Another Pagon idolatress goddess birthed from the infamous Pagan Roman Catholic Tradition. Cathlic.com in their discreditable definition describes the reason why they hailed Mary (Birth Mother of Jesus) as the Queen of Heaven to be adorned, serviced and worshiped. This very popular pagan practice evolved in or around the Middle Ages. Its theological basis derived from the notion of Jesus as King. The New Testament uses the image of a "King" to describe Jesus in Israel. The mother of the king held the role of "Queen Mother". In essence she held a role of great prominence in the court and the king would usually willingly accommodate her wishes. In **1 and 2 Kings** the kings are almost always listed with their mothers and were depicted as advising their sons. As Jesus is king, they {The Catholic Church} self-justifies Mary as his queen mother according to Jewish {Pagon} tradition. Getting to the king through the "Queen Mother" (and not Jesus) is a natural thought and spurred {non-believers & those ignorant to God's word} to ask Mary {A Mere Mortal Dead Human Being} to intercede with Jesus on their behalf {Blasphemy}. They go on to sight, Mary's queenship is a share in Jesus' kingship.

This distorted, perverted false pagan theology is why I urge you to at all cost, question by way of the scriptures, what is being forced down your throat. You must test the fruits and assure it is from God before receiving, before agreeing, or coming in any type of alignment with it. The word commands that you test the spirits, see **1 John 4** " *Beloved, do not believe every spirit, but test the spirits to see whether they are from God, for many false prophets have gone out into the world. By this you know the Spirit of God: every spirit that confesses that Jesus Christ has come in the flesh is from God, and every spirit that does not confess Jesus is not from God. This is the spirit of the antichrist, which you heard was coming and now is in the world already.*" Bowing down to, worshiping or serving any idol or anything that can be made an idol is a sacrilege in the eyes of God. See **Exodus 20:5**

"You shall not bow down to them or worship them; for I, the Lord your God, am a jealous God…"
Exodus 20:5

In the 4ᵗʰ century "Paganism" was derived from the Roman Empire for those who openly practiced polytheism. Wikipedia describes "Polytheism as the belief in multiple deities {gods}, which are usually assembled into a pantheon of gods and goddesses, along with their own religious sects and rituals. It contrasts with monotheism, the belief in a one singular God {Yahweh}." Thus, the seed of witchcraft being formed. There is only one God, one Son and one Holy Spirit. His words clearly state that no one shall worship idol gods for no particular reason, there is only one God.

See **Leviticus 26:1** *"You shall not make for yourselves idols, nor shall you set up for yourselves an image or a sacred pillar, nor shall you place a figured stone in your land to bow down to it; for I am the Lord your God.* **Exodus 20:3-6** *"You shall have no other gods before me.* <u>*You shall not make for yourself an idol, or any likeness*</u> *of what is in heaven above or on the earth beneath or in the water under the earth. You shall not worship them or serve them; for I, the Lord your God, am a jealous God, visiting the iniquity of the fathers on the children, on the third and the fourth generations* *of those who hate."* **Jonah 2:8** "Those who regard vain idols forsake their faithfulness". **Psalm 135:15** "The idols of the nations are but silver and gold, the work of man's hands." **Isaiah 45:20** "They have no knowledge, who carry about their wooden idol and pray to a god who cannot save." **Revelation 9:20** "The rest of mankind, who were not killed by these plagues, did not repent of the works of their hands, so as not to worship demons, and the idols of gold and of silver and of brass and of stone and of wood, which can neither see nor hear nor walk;" **Micah 5:13** *"I will cut off your carved images and your sacred pillars from among you, so that you will no longer bow down to the work of your hands."* **Jeremiah 1:16** *I will pronounce my judgments on them concerning all their wickedness, whereby they have forsaken me and have offered sacrifices to other gods, and* worshiped the works of their own hands." **Habakkuk 2:18** "What profit is the idol when its maker has carved it, or an image, a teacher of falsehood? For its maker trusts in his own handiwork when he fashions speechless idols." **Jeremiah 7; 18** "The children gather wood, the fathers kindle the fire, and the women knead the dough, to make cakes for the queen of heaven, and they pour out drink offerings to other gods, that may provoke me to anger."

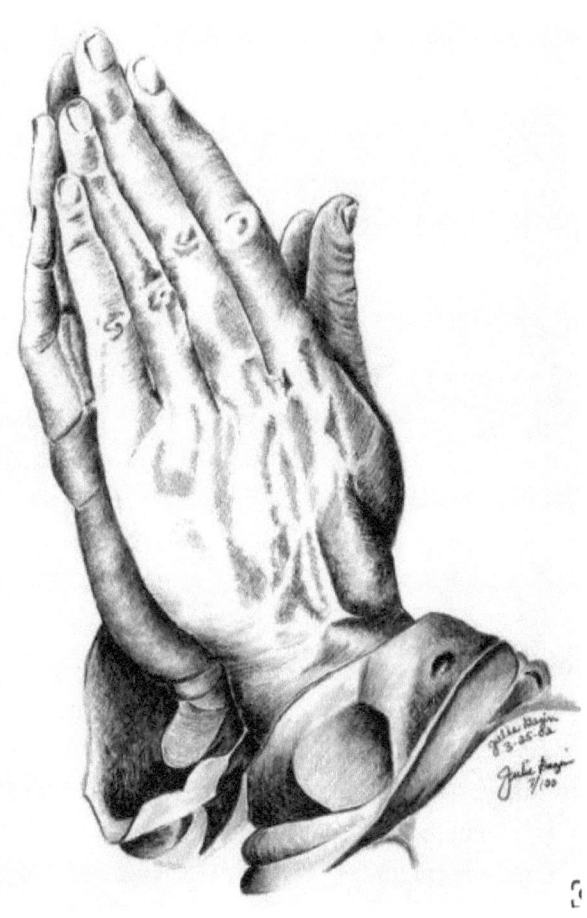

SPIRITUAL REPOSSESSION
TAKING IT ALL BACK

1 Samuel 30:8 "So David inquired of the Lord, saying, "Shall I pursue this troop? Shall I overtake them?" And He answered him, "Pursue", for you shall surely overtake them and without fail, recover all." In this present time, we live in a spiritual atmosphere where metaphorically we can be "spiritually robbed" at any time. The believer and the non-believer alike has to be sober minded, alert and on guard because sleeping on our enemy can be very costly, even unto the point of death or our soul. Inversely there will be times and circumstances where you have to be a "willing vessel". That's willing to get up, get dressed, and go into the enemy's camp and Spiritually Repossess what was stolen from you, e.g., a rape victim, self- worth. A drug addict, their sobriety. Mental illness, a peace of mind. Heart-broken wife, self-love or possibly the ability of learning to love again. Abandoned child, strength, strength to overcome, forgive and become a generational curse

breaker who's willing to change the game. These things on certain occasions must be taken back. Our enemy the adversary will never be willingly standing by with these vital elements of life he has stolen saying " Does this belong to you; would you like it back?" You have to plead the blood of Jesus over your life in order to be covered ,you must pray for permission and protection over your journey. You must put your war clothes on and be willing to go into the enemy's camp and reclaim all the devil has robbed & abducted. **Deuteronomy 20 1 "**When thou goest out to battle against thine enemies, and seest horses, and chariots, and a people more than thou, be not afraid of them: for the Lord thy God is with thee,". **Joshua 1:9 "**Have I not commanded you? Be strong and courageous. Do not be afraid; do not be discouraged, for the Lord your God will be with you wherever you go". These six elements to appropriate "Spiritual Repossession" are as follows.

The Six Elements of a
"Spiritual Repossession."

1. Pray & Rebuke (simple demons)
2. Prayer & Fasting (stubborn demons)
3. Spiritual Disinfection (house cleaning) Spiritual House & Physical House.
4. Seeking "God's Permission" for a recovery
5. Faith/Belief (unseen things of God)
6. Binding Loosing (Warring in the Spirit)

1) Pray & Rebuke (simple demons)

James 5 16*"The effectual fervent prayer of a righteous man availeth much."* Pray and call the demon out by name or names, call out the manifestations); then demand firmly in the name of, the Lord Jesus Christ that they/it leaves. Bind the evil spirit in the name of Jesus. Loose warring Spirits of intercession. Loose the Army of God and Be Loosed.

2) Prayer & Fasting (stubborn demons)

Certain stubborn demons passed down through cycles or generational curses can only be driven out by way of prayer and fasting. These types of demons set up shop for the "Territory". They are territorial demons that have been a family for decades, they are always looking for the next victim or generation to work through, they are comfortable , they have plenty of turf to seize other souls, these types of satanic imps don't plan on going anywhere, they have to been driven out by demolishing spells and breaking generation curses by way of prayer and fasting.

3) Spiritual Disinfection (house cleaning) of Spiritual House & Physical House.

Items that can bring a curse under your house. If you discover that you have been harboring these things in your house, they should probably be disposed of immediately.

- Evil Jewelry
- Evil Art or Pictures
- Wood Carven Images from
- Africa or Haiti
- Tarot Cards/ Crystal Balls
- Ouija Boards
- Idolatrous statues/dolls,
- Buddha, carved bulls, lucifer, porcelain cows or goats.
- Evil Books, Pornography or Magazines
- Trunks, cases, urns used to house occultic paraphernalia.
- Occultic Paraphernalia, Games , cards books
- Good luck charms & satanic symbols
- Certain satanic Hip Hop and Heavy metal Records or CD's
- Crystals used for Rituals & Spells
- Incense (Sage) burned to other Gods
- Used furniture and tables used for sacrifice or evil altars

4) Seeking "God's Permission" for Recovery

1 Samuel 30:8 "*And David inquired at the LORD, saying, Shall I pursue after this troop? shall I overtake them? And he answered him, Pursue: for thou shalt surely overtake them, and without fail recover all*" It is crucial that seeks Gods Permission to recover what was stolen from you. That the "Helper i.e. The Holy Spirit" will guide in all Spiritual Wisdom Truth and Prudence. You don't need a mediator that's why Jesus sent forth his beloved Holy Spirit in the World. The **WHAT** is not always as important as the **HOW.** It was only after David sought **Gods PERMISSION** was he able to **"Recover ALL"**

5) Faith/Belief (unseen things of God)

Jesus looked at his disciples and said "Only Believe" this is a spiritual fight. I caution you the invisible war is very much real and has the ability to sniff out fear like a dog. Fear paralyzes faith as well as your efforts to overcome the binding holds of spiritual manipulation and witchcraft. Know and understand that you are just the vessel in which God will perform his power.

6) Binding Loosing (Warring in the Spirit)

It is vital for us to learn to exercise "Legal kingdom Authority" to bind evil spirits, and also to loose the spirits of God in order to be freed and loosed **(Matthew 18:18),** 1 John 4:4, Hebrews 1:7, 14). It is not complicated. Deliverance Pastor Win Worley gives an example of a simple prayer: "I take authority over the spirits of {name them} in {name of person}, in the name of the Lord Jesus Christ.

But those who hope in the LORD will renew their strength. They will soar on wings like eagles; they will run and not grow weary, they will walk and not be faint.
Isaiah 40:31

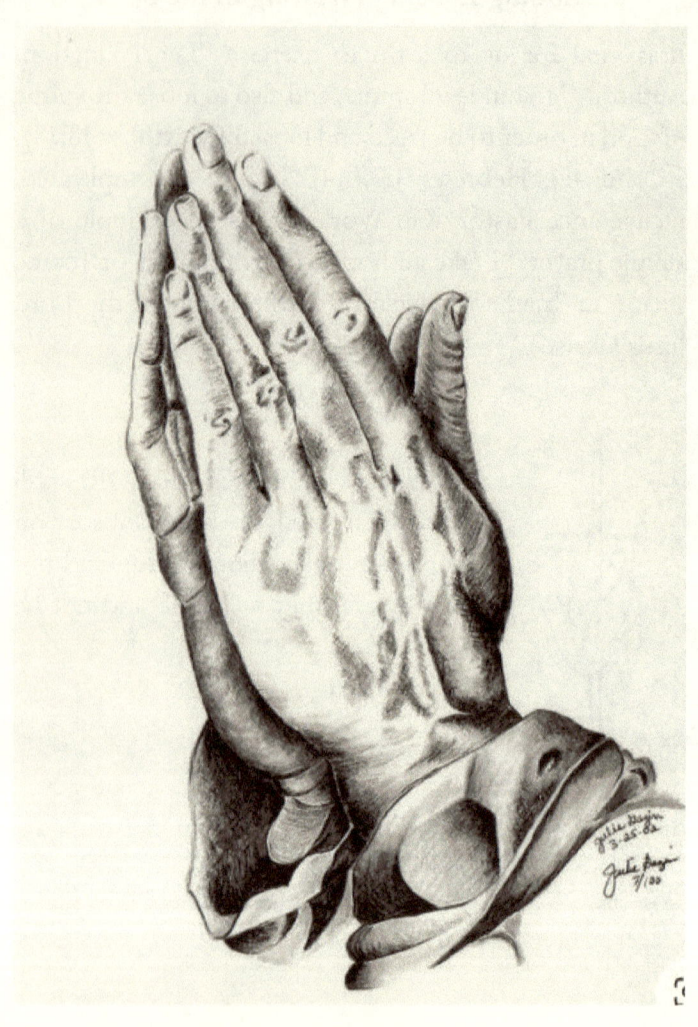

Job 22:28

DECREES OVER EVIL ENTANGLEMENTS

J ob **22 28** "You will also declare a thing, And it will be established for you; So light will shine on your ways." A decree is a legal proclamation issued by a head of state, according to certain procedures. It enforces the law. A decree is an official order that is drafted and issued by someone in a position of legal authority. "Decree" means a law, order, fiat or edict. In the Kingdom of God legal decrees are and can be issued by legal citizens of the kingdom of heaven. People possessing kingdom authority. **Luke 10:19** "Behold, I have given you authority to tread on serpents and scorpions, and over all the power of the enemy, and nothing shall hurt you." **Deuteronomy 4:6** Observe them carefully, because this will show your wisdom and discernment in the eyes of people who'll listen to all these decrees. Then they'll say: "Surely this great nation is a wise and discerning people.' **John 16:13** "When the Spirit of truth comes, he will guide you into all the truth, for he will not speak on his own authority, but whatever he hears he will speak, and he will declare to you the things that are to come**." Luke 9:1**"And he called the twelve together and gave them power and authority over all demons and to cure diseases."

An evil decree is a satanic pronouncement or curses issued on an individual or group of persons from a satanic altar by a satanic personality with authority. Such a person can be a witch doctor, warlock, voodoo priest or priestess, occultist or satanist, false prophet, false teacher etc. When such pronouncement is made, the evil spiritual assignment is quickly assigned to and supervised by a demon or group of demons (satanic magistrates). They are negative assertions or satanic false prophecies . The evil decree can be likened to a satanic barrier placed within the victim's path.

The good news is that our enemy has no power to kill us, if he did most of us would probably be dead by now. The blood of Jesus still protects, heals and delivers see **Exodus 12:13** – *"The blood shall be to you for a token (sign) upon the houses where you are: and when I see the blood, I will pass over you, and the plague shall not be upon you to destroy you when I smite the land of Egypt."* It is imperative that you "Plead the Blood of Jesus" over all that God has made you steward over, including but not limited to your life, health, home, marriage, children, finances, future etc. Also, there is a redeemer that the "redeemed of the Lord shall say so" **Acts 2 35** *'The Lord said to my Lord, "Sit at My right hand, Till I make Your enemies Your footstool. "Therefore,* *let all the house of Israel know assuredly that God has made this Jesus, whom you crucified, both Lord and Christ."*

There are divine decrees that can overrule any satanic verdict or decree issued. **Matthew 4:10**

"Then saith Jesus unto him, Get thee behind me, Satan: for it is written, Thou shalt worship the Lord thy God, and him only shalt thou serve". ***1 John 3 8*** *"Whoever makes a practice of sinning is of the devil, for the devil has been sinning from the beginning. The reason the Son of God appeared was to destroy the works of the devil.* ***Colossians 2 14-15*** *"By canceling the record of debt that stood against us with its legal demands. This he set aside, nailing it to the cross. He disarmed the rulers and authorities and put them to open shame, by triumphing over them in him.* **2 Corinthians 4:4** *"In their case the god of this world has blinded the minds of the unbelievers, to keep them from seeing the light of the gospel of the glory of Christ, who is the image of God."* **Romans 8:28** *"And we know that all things work together for good to them that love God, to them who are called according to his purpose".* **Hebrew 12 12** *"Looking to Jesus, the founder and perfecter of our faith, who for the joy that was set before him endured the cross, despising the shame, and is seated at the right hand of the throne of God".*

The 7 Decrees against "Satanic Evil Entanglements"

I Decree and Declare

1. That any lying, gossiping accusatory tongue that rises up against me or my family in judgment, slander or gossip you God shall condemn

I Decree and Declare

2. Any evil satanic covenants or contracts legal or illegal written against me at any evil altar to hurt, harm, frustrate or destroy me or family is hereby, nullified, voided and to no effect by the Blood of Christ. With the sword of God, I sever them.

I Decree and Declare

3. That I renounce any Un-Godly association that may have opened the door to evil satanic possession, interference or Ungodly Soul Ties. I repent of my sin, submit to the will of God and resist the devil. He must flee. Though he came in one way the Spirit of the Lord scatters him in six different ways.

I Decree and Declare

4. That I can do all things through Christ Jesus who strengthens me. For greater is HE that is in me than he that is in this world. All generational curses and wicked cycles tied to the chains of worthless and profitless tradition are hereby severed. I sever them by the sword of the Spirit and Destroy them by the Blood of Christ our risen Messiah

I Decree and Declare

5. That the victory Christ Jesus won at the cross is sufficient. Jesus paid it all. Therefore, I reject and resist any evil endeavors of Satan that will rob me of

the will of God. I will take my place with him the heavenlies until he makes every one of my enemies my footstool.

I Decree and Declare

6. That God makes to Triumph Always. I am fearfully and wonderfully made; I am the head and not the tail. I am Fearlessly victorious over every enemy of my soul. You pour out fresh anointing from heaven's window, that yokes are hereby destroyed. Any trap that the enemy sets for me that is set for me shall also be the ones my enemies fall in with the angel of the Lord perusing and devouring them. You shall strike demonic forces down in the midst of their own mischief and their mischief is multiplied unto them, 3-fold.

I Decree and Declare

7. I will operate in my anointing using all power and Authority against the forces of hell that attempt to take over my life. The anointing breaks the Yoke and destroys every fetter . You have given me "Power" and Authority to trample over snakes, scorpions and over all manner of evil and by no means shall it harm ME. I Plead the blood of Jesus over me and against them. The devil is defeated, God is exalted and today victory is mine. Be lifted up Oh Ye Gates and the king of Glory shall come in.

Luke 10:19

POWER AND AUTHORITY OVER ALL OF SATANIC FORCES OF HELL

Ephesians 4 11-12 *"So Christ himself gave the apostles, the prophets, the evangelists, the pastors and teachers, to equip his people for works of service, so that the body of Christ may be built up until we all reach unity in the faith and in the knowledge of the Son of God and become mature, attaining to the whole measure of the fullness of Christ.* **1 Corinthians 4 20-** *"For the kingdom of God is not in word but in power".* **Acts 4 31** *"And when they had prayed, the place where they were assembled together was shaken; and they were all filled with the Holy Spirit, and they spoke the word of God with boldness."* **Acts 1 8** *"But you shall receive power when the Holy Spirit has come upon you; and you shall be witnesses to Me in Jerusalem, and in all Judea and Samaria, and to the end of the earth."* **2 Corinthians 10 3-** *"For though we walk in the flesh, we do not war according to the flesh. For the weapons of our warfare are not carnal but mighty through God to the pulling down of strong holds; Casting down*

imaginations, and every high thing that exalteth itself against the knowledge of God, and bringing into captivity every thought to the obedience of Christ,"

Ephesians 1:20-21 " *He exerted when he raised Christ from the dead and seated him at his right hand in the heavenly realms, far above all rule and authority, power and dominion, and every name that is invoked, not only in the present age but also in the one to come."* **Ephesians 2: 19** *"So then you are no longer strangers and aliens, but you are fellow citizens with the saints, and are of God's household"*, **Philippians 3:20** *"For our citizenship is in heaven, from which also we eagerly wait for a Savior, the Lord Jesus Christ"* **Peter 1:4** *"To obtain an inheritance which is imperishable and undefiled and will not fade away, reserved in heaven for you."*

By the emphatical, unshakable, unbreakable Word of God the "Covenant Believer", the true kingdom citizens have legally inherited , " Power and Authority" over every area and every situation of their life, but if you don't use it what good is it. It is like sitting on a loaded pistol that you "don't" or "don't know how" to effectively use it. We don't accept defeat nor do we bow down to excuses. God has equipped us with everything we need in the world not only to fight but also to win and be victorious. This is an endurance race where the prize is only granted to one winner. You have to run this spiritual race of life with the utmost endurance and do not faint. Refuse to faint. While running for your life, declare to all the forces of hell you are "in it to win it" and you shall not faint. Fainting is not an option, that's what the enemy wants you to do. He knows that if you ever got loose. If you ever decided to walk in your true purpose, you would be an ultimate threat to him. We serve a God that makes us triumph. **Psalm 27 13-14** "*I would have fainted, unless I had believed that I would see the goodness of the Lord in the land of the living.*"

The road to overcoming spiritual manipulation will not be easy. Please don't read this book and say Mya said! it will be all bunnies and roses once you come to Christ seeking redemption, and refunds from the enemy because it definitely will not, but I can guarantee it will be worth it, once you have endured to the end.

We serve a God that can do anything but fail. Below here I list the 7 Kingdom tools you will need to utilize as your first steps in using your power and authority over all of the forces of hell. The Kingdom of God didn't come to play, we came to slay everything standing with no intention of leaving anything behind. See **Revelation 20 7-10** "*And when the thousand years are ended, Satan will be released from his prison and will come out to <u>deceive the nations</u> that are at the four corners of the earth, Gog and Magog, to gather them for battle; their number is like the sand of the sea. And they marched up over the broad plain of the earth and surrounded the camp of the saints and the beloved city, <u>but fire came down from heaven and consumed them,</u> and the devil who had deceived them was thrown into the lake of fire and sulfur where the beast and the false prophet were, and they will be tormented day and night forever and ever*". When the enemy reminds you of your past, it is imperative to remind him of his future.

The 7 Kingdom tools that you need to "overcome" are listed as...

- ➤ God's Word
  The Sword of the Spirit
- ➤ Decrees & Declaration
  Legal Proclamation
- ➤ Faith over Fear
  Believing with an Expectancy
- ➤ Praying And Fasting
  To Drive out Stubborn Demons
- ➤ Warring in the "Spirit"
  Fighting the invisible "Spiritual Battle in the Word (Full Armor of God)
- ➤ Binding & Loosing
  Binding evil taunting spirits and loosing ministering Spirits (The Army of God)
- ➤ Spiritual Repossession
  Taking back everything the devil has stole by way of legal authority.

LEGAL KINGDOM RIGHTS

All things work together for the good of those who love, serve and keep God's commandments. Every intricate part of man's redemption from sin, precisely follows an elaborate, historical, lawful step by step procedure, pathing the way for Legal Kingdom Rights for the citizens of the kingdom of heaven; that is the eviction of satan from heaven, the fall of man in the Garden of Eden from sin, until the crucifixion and the resurrection of Jesus Christ notwithstanding the final closing act. The Return of Christ the redeemer to defeat our enemies of darkness. Lucifer the devil, the beast and the false prophet who sets out to deceive the nations. Having redeemed mankind from sin, we became beneficiaries of a heavenly inheritance.

As an obedient covenant believer, you are a legal citizen not a foreign citizen, not a refugee or an illegal alien of the kingdom of God. You have a right to everything that the Kingdom has to offer! if you don't forfeit. There is a judicial covenant between Jesus and God, signed in Jesus' blood, which provides these rights for you. **Matthew 16:19** "*I will give you the keys of the kingdom of heaven; whatever you bind on earth will be bound in heaven, and whatever you loose on earth will be loosed in heaven.*"(Romans 8:17). Our position as children of God and joint heirs with Jesus are the laws of the Kingdom of God ,being legally binding to establish , protect and preserve the benefits and privileges for its kingdom citizens.

The 7 Legal Rights to Citizens of The Kingdom

1. You Have the Right to Be Free

"Therefore, if the Son makes you free, you shall be free indeed."
–John 8:36 (NKJV)

2. You Have the Right to Be Healed

"By His stripes we are healed."
–Isaiah 53:5 (NKJV)

3. The Right to Repentance unto forgiveness

Romans 3 20-24
But now the righteousness of God without the law is manifested, being witnessed by the law and the prophets;
Even the righteousness of God which is by faith of Jesus

<u>Christ unto all and upon all them that believe: for there
is no difference: For all have sinned, and come short of
the glory of God; Being justified freely by his grace
through the redemption that is in Christ Jesus:</u>

4. You Have the Right to "Fearless Living"

"For you did not receive the spirit of bondage again to
fear, but you received the Spirit of adoption by whom we
cry out, 'Abba, Father.'"
–Romans 8:15 (NKJV)

5. You Have the Right to Have Peace

"The Lord will bless His people with peace."
–Psalm 29:11

6. You Have the Right to Access and utilize the Name of Jesus

"And this is his command: to believe in the name of his
Son, Jesus Christ." –1 John 3:23 Luke 10 17 The seventy-
two returned with joy and said, "Lord, even the demons
submit to us in your name."

7. You Have the Right to Always Triumph

"Now thanks be unto God, which always causeth us to
triumph in Christ."
–2 Corinthians 2:14 (KJV)

Pray without Ceasing

Suffer no Identity Crises in the Lord. Know who you are in the Kingdom. Know your established legal right in the Kingdom of God. Bind and Loose. Put on the Full Armor of God that you will be able to resist the wiles of the devil and take a stand against the enemies' scams

Praise God even in the moments of harsh realities and unknown mysteries. Speak! Speak the word of Jesus. Power of life and death lies in your own tongue, the power to bind and loose. Be worded up, this is not a physical war, this is a spiritual war. Your sword in the word of God. Develop a radical trust without borders . Know who you are in the Kingdom. Know your established legal right and rank in the Kingdom of God. Bind and loose. Submit to the will of God and resist the devil he will flee. Time to fight back. Clothes mouths don't get fed on earth or in the Kingdom of God. If you are not experienced or confident in the realm of Spiritual Warfare, pray for intercession.

Ephesians 5:12

POWER OVER SPIRITUAL MANIPULATION

Spiritual Manipulation, this is the part where we get real and real serious. **Matthew 5 13** *"Believer, you are the salt of the earth; but if the salt loses its flavor, how shall it be seasoned? It is then good for nothing but to be thrown out and trampled underfoot by men."*

This is where we expose some fake churches, some false prophets and prophetess, disturbed sexual predators fronting in the Name of Jesus, evangelical witch doctors, false teachers and wolves in sheep's clothing. **Matthew 10.16** *"Behold, I send you forth as sheep in the midst of wolves: be ye therefore wise as serpents, and harmless as doves."* **Matthew 7 13** *"broad is the way, that leadeth to destruction"*, **Matthew 24 4** *"And Jesus answered and said to them: "Take heed that no one deceives you. For many will come in My name, saying, 'I am the Christ,' and will deceive many"*. **Colossians 2-8** *"Beware lest anyone cheat you through philosophy and empty deceit, according to* *the tradition of men, according to the basic principles of the world, and not according to Christ".*

Taking your life, health, strength, spirituality, mental wellbeing and sexuality back from the enemy heavily revolves around the characteristics of bold ,affirmative, renunciation and identification. You first have to identify the persons, place or force, then it is imperative to renounce any ungodly allegiances, oaths or soul ties that one has come in contact with knowingly or unknowingly.

Super-Wiki (an occultic version of Wikipedia) recites **Spiritual {Witchcraft} manipulation** as "To create, shape and manipulate spiritual energy or forces. Spiritual energy is commonly associated with the energy of a sentient being's soul, or places with spiritual influence either by spiritual beings like ghosts or other supernatural phenomena. Typically, users can use spiritual energy as a sixth sense (demonic), materializing it into a physical form to unleash attacks, or becoming intangible like actual spirits." **Ezekial 34:1-4** *"The word of the Lord came to me: "Son of man, prophesy against the shepherds of Israel; prophesy, and say to them, even to the shepherds, Thus says the Lord God: Ah, shepherds of Israel who have been feeding yourselves! Should not shepherds feed the sheep? You eat the fat, you clothe yourselves with the wool, you slaughter the fat ones, but you do not feed the sheep. The weak you have not strengthened, the sick you have not healed, the injured you have not bound up, the strayed you have not brought back, the lost you have not sought, and with force and harshness you have ruled them."*

Kingdom Complications defines **Spiritual Manipulation through preaching** as "Seeking to change the perception or behavior of others through underhanded, deceptive, or even abusive tactics instead of teaching the Scriptures {or God's Holy Law}. **Narcissistic Manipulation** is when an extremely self-centered individual possessing an inflated sense of self-importance, strategies and behaviors deceitfully and deceptively uses another person to gain power, prosperity, influence, dominance and control over those individuals or their lives. We will differentiate the character traits between the three.

Spiritual {Witchcraft} manipulation

> ➢ "Sixth Sense"
> ➢ White magic
> ➢ Black magic
> ➢ Sorcery
> ➢ Tarot Card
> ➢ Voodoo, Hoodoo
> ➢ Santeria
> ➢ Ouija Boards
> ➢ Numerology
> ➢ Astrology
> ➢ Spells

Spiritual Manipulation
through preaching

➤ "Seeds For Sale" Selling a "Spiritual Seed" for material gain, wealth or any other self-indulged reason

➤ Bullying, intimidation or shaming from the pulpit

➤ Twisting the "word of God" to justify gross criminal behavior such as, sexual harassment fornication or sexual abuse with in Church

➤ Sexual Exploitation and Abuse among Pastors , Church Goers Popes or Clergymen

➤ Twisting the Scriptures for Spiritual, Political, Monetary Gain

➤ Lukewarm Prosperity message that constantly boast about the desire of wealth and never warns about the consequences of sin , hell or rebelling against God

➤ Vivid imaginations and allegories that corrupt themselves against the true knowledge of God.

➤ "Lying on God" Prophesying in one's own name. False Phropetism

➤ Stealing, Embezzling, Conning, Hustling, manipulating and using Sermons and scriptures to abed in the thievery

➢ Using sermons as instruments to formulate occultic sects openly or on the down low.

Narcissistic Manipulation

- ➢ Lying
- ➢ Hating
- ➢ Bullying
- ➢ Gossiping
- ➢ Stealing
- ➢ Exploitation
- ➢ Intimidation
- ➢ Brain Washing
- ➢ Accusatory Attacks
- ➢ Extreme Selfishness
- ➢ No Accountability
- ➢ Victim Mentality
- ➢ Secret Atheistic Beliefs
- ➢ Outburst of Anger
- ➢ Assassination of Character
- ➢ Instigator of Trouble
- ➢ Violent Reactions
- ➢ Inflictors of Emotional Pain
- ➢ Frustrating or attempting to frustrate the Plans of God, its Prophets or the People of God

Jeremiah 5 30-31 God rebuked false prophets through Jeremiah saying *"An astonishing and horrible thing Has been committed in the land: The prophets prophesy falsely, the priests rule by their own power; And My people love to have it so. But what will you do in the end?* **Matt 23** stated *"<u>For they preach, but do not practice</u>. They tie up heavy burdens, hard to bear, and lay them on people's shoulders, <u>but they themselves are not willing to move them with their finger</u>... So you also outwardly appear righteous to others, but within you are full of hypocrisy and lawlessness."* **Jude 12&13** *"These are hidden reefs at your love feasts, as they feast with you without fear, shepherds feeding themselves; waterless clouds, swept along by winds; fruitless trees in late autumn, twice dead, uprooted; wild waves of the sea, casting up the foam of their own shame; wandering stars, for whom the gloom of utter darkness has been reserved forever."* John in **1 John 4.1** *"Dear friends, do not believe every spirit, but test the spirits to see whether they are from God, because many false prophets have gone out into the world."* **James 4:7** *"Therefore submit to God. Resist the devil and he will flee from you. For these false teachers, hypocrites and false prophets possess "a form" of godliness, denying the power thereof. From such people or persons do not be afraid to turn away".*

Over Come

You overcome these types of manipulations by equaling works with faith and utilizing the kingdom tools of "Power and Authority" that Jesus left for you to use! We are the head and not the tail. We are above and not beneath. We don't have to fear these forces, they should be fearing us! **1 Peter 2:9** *"But ye are a chosen generation, a royal priesthood, a holy nation, a peculiar people; that ye should shew forth the praises of him who hath called you out of darkness into his marvelous light".* Your most vital tools are.

1. Wisdom/ Discernment
2. Knowledge of Scriptures. Reading & Understanding of God's Word
3. Earnest Prayer
4. Courage to Speak boldly and even walk away
5. Bind the Strong-Hold of the Enemy

KINGDOM AUTHORITY

Ephesians 1:18 *"I pray that the eyes of your understanding may be enlightened in order that you may know the hope to which he has called you, the riches of his glorious inheritance in his holy people"*. **1 Peter 2-9** *"But you are a chosen people, a royal priesthood, a holy nation, God's special possession, that you may declare the praises of him who called you out of darkness into his wonderful light"*. **1 John 4 4-** *"Greater is he that is in you, than he that is in the world."* **Romans 8 18** *"the sufferings of this present time are not worthy to be compared with the glory which shall be revealed in us"*. **Job 13 15-17** *"Though He slay me, yet will I trust Him"*.

Today we put on the new man of Jesus Christ. We boldly take a stand against the devil's scams that have been prevailing in our lives for way to long. We will clarify this "Kingdom Authority" thing and settle the debate here and now.

All Power and Authority in Heaven and in Earth **BELONG TO JESUS CHRIST,** satan is a temporary month to month lease holder. **Matthew 4- 8-10** *"Again,* *the devil took Him up on an exceedingly high mountain, and showed Him all the kingdoms of the world and their glory. And he said to Him, "All these things I will give you if you will fall down and worship me." Then Jesus said to him, "Away with you, Satan!* __*For it is written, 'You shall worship the Lord your God, and Him only you shall serve.*__" He, Jesus who is the Christ, is the head of ALL things and it is (He alone) who holds the keys to the Kingdom in his hands. No man gets to the father except through Jesus Christ, not by charity donations, not by good works, not by going to Church every Sunday, not by feeding the poor, tithing or fighting for civil rights. There are a whole lot of lovers of God but very few lovers of his son Jesus. Many have been deceived but unto the covenant believer there is a "Blessed Assurance". Unto those who are children of God by first right and adoption, they have obtained legal citizenship of the kingdom as "Children of God". **Romans 8:17** *'Now if we are children, then we are heirs—heirs of God and co-heirs with Christ. As Christ heirs (Confession Christ as Messiah, keeping his law and commandments). We have the right to discipleship which gives us access to (Utilize) this kingdom Power and Authority "in the Heavenlies".* **Matthew 28 18-20** *"And Jesus came and spoke to them, saying, "All authority has been given to Me in heaven and on earth. Go therefore and make disciples of all the nations, baptizing them in the name of the Father and of the Son and of the Holy Spirit, teaching them to observe all things that I have commanded you; and lo, I am with you always, even to the end of the age. Amen."*

The things that they (Christ Disciples) taught us about using this Power and Authority were to fight, war and repossess that which was stolen, in the heavenlies.

These seven tools are what you need to take an adequate stance in using your Power and Authority over every enemy of your soul. These tools will assure that your warfare prayer is bold, effectual, and fervent. For the effectual fervent prayer of the righteous "availeth" much.

> ➤ **Repentance (Repent with Godly Sorrow & Full Surrender)**

1. Willingly Repent with Godly Sorrow for anything that you have done in deed, thought or action knowing or unknowingly. You can not expect a Prayer to be effectual, holding onto bitterness, resentment and unforgiveness against anyone. Forgiveness frees you not them. Unforgiveness will void your prayer and paralyze your efforts. Many wonder why their prayers seem as if they are not being answered. Those are typically narcissistic individuals or people who won't acknowledge their own accountability, never forgiving or able to forgive.

> ➤ **Rebuke**

2. The King James Dictionary defines rebuke as "To reprimand; strongly warn; restrain. **Titus 2 15** "Speak these things, **exhort, and rebuke with all authority.** Let no one despise you." The reason why it is imperative to rebuke curses (spoken, casted or

generational) is because if you willingly come into agreement or alignment with any evil offense, dark force or curse it becomes yours. When you open up your mouth with Holy Boldness and have no fear to bind that spoken transgression with rebuke, it becomes nullified rendering no effect. That thing that has been, or attempting to come against you is hereby reprimanded through Jesus with full Kingdom Authority and will be restrained and bound up for you to cast out. Its decision is interrupted because you are entering in your legal "spiritual appeal" in the kingdom with your rebuke. Never willingly accept a negative opinion, spoken word or a curse over your life. You can rebuke a verbal curse by simply saying "I don't agree with that or I DON'T receive that. For obvious demon possession you are demanding that it leave or be cast out

> **Renounce**

3. Renunciation of any Ungodly association or soul tie is essential. Sometimes we have come into Ungodly allegiances or Soul Ties "Un knowingly". Probably that time you read the horoscope and identified with a sign. Secretly agreeing to a secret oath (sorority, secret society or contract oath), Worshiped idol gods through a song ritual, not knowing because it was written in secret code played backwards. It could be that individual you have dated in the past, who was practicing voodoo and sacrificing cats in chickens in

his mama's basement. Just to name a few. These are end time realities happening every day in plain sight. Willfully renounce any possible occurrence knowingly and unknowingly.

➤ **BIND**

4. **Matthew 12 29** "how can one enter a strong man's house and plunder his goods, unless he first binds the strong man" Demons have to be Bound in order to be stopped, stop them from playing with your mind and wreaking havoc in your life. Demons fear and tremble at the name of Jesus."

➤ **Loose**

5. When the disciples "loose" something, or allowed it on earth, the releasing of something or someone the enemy has had "bound -up" often refers to the loosing of a captive or person in bondage. You bind demons, and you loose the captives that have been held prisoner to the enemy's trickery. When Jesus set free the woman with the issue of blood, He said unto her, "Woman, thou art loosed from thine infirmity." (Luke 13:12)

➤ **Release**

6. Believe with the Utmost conviction that is done! Release any questions or mysteries beyond your understanding into his hands. **Matthew 11 28** "Come

to Me, all you who labor and are heavy laden, and I will give you rest. Take My yoke upon you and learn from Me." **John 14 1** "Do not let your hearts be troubled. You believe in God; believe also in me". **Mark 1 15** "The time has come," he said. "The kingdom of God has come near. Repent and believe the good news!" **Mark 9 23"** If you can'?" said Jesus. "Everything is possible for one who believes. **Mark 11 24** Therefore I tell you, whatever you ask for in prayer, believe that you have received it, and it will be yours"** Believe that it is done. Thank Him before the manifestation of the Blessing. Release the issue into Jesus' all powerful hands give it to the King. Knowing that it is DONE!

Conclusion!

To the faithful, obedient, covenant believer you have to know that you are "Kingdom Royalty". The head and not the tail, you are above and not beneath. Your Blessed Assurance rests in the Kingdom of God not the opinions or evaluation of man. If God be for you that's better than the whole world against you. Man does not ordain what your future will hold, God does. Jesus paid it all from the cradle, cross to the grave to reserve your dwelling place in his heavenly estate. He paid a debt that we could never afford to pay so that the gift of salvation would not be stolen from us. From the cradle to the grave, his presence served the most meaningful reason for being. Your eternal life, your soul, your mansion, your purpose driven existence and "Yes", you do have a Purpose. Regardless of the lies spoken to you and maybe even over you. We serve a "Living Risen Savior". We don't serve a gold-plated statue from Walmart. The keys to the Kingdom are in "His" hands. Outside of the Unpardonable Sin which is Blaspheming the Holy Spirit. There is no satanic trickery, entrapment, coercion, seduction, forms of witchcraft, deception, spiritual manipulation interference, nor possession that can't be overturned by "Renunciation and Repentance". HE IS A LIAR! Whom the Son set s free is free indeed. The heavens rejoice when one of his lost sheep returns home. **Acts 26:18** *"to open their eyes so that they may turn from darkness to light and from the dominion of Satan to God, that they may receive forgiveness of sins and an inheritance among those who have been sanctified by faith in Me".* **Psalm 107:10** *"There were those who dwelt in darkness and in the shadow of death, Prisoners in misery and chains".* **Colossians 1:13,** *"For He rescued us from the domain of darkness, and transferred us to the kingdom of His beloved Son".* **Ephesians 5:8** *"for you were formerly darkness, but now you are Light in the Lord; walk as children of the Light".* **1 Peter 2-9** *"But you are a chosen generation, a royal priesthood, a holy nation, His own special people, that you may proclaim the praises of Him who called you out of darkness into His marvelous light".* **2 Chronicles 7:14** *"If my people who are called by my name will humble themselves, and pray and seek my face, and turn from their wicked ways, then I will hear from heaven, and will forgive their sin and heal their land".*

There is kingdom power to help you, reverse the curse, break the spell and emotional hindrance over your life. No one is too bad and no one is too far gone from God's Grace. If that was the case, I wouldn't be here alive to write this book today. The devil, our enemy doesn't want you loose from bondage. He knows if you ever got clean, if you ever overcame, if you ever became spiritually free you would be a "Mighty Force that would change the game". As the Father welcomed home an estranged prodigal son. So, with repentance will our Heavenly Father welcome you. We overcome by the Blood of the Lamb, the confessions, our testimony, repentance and effectual prayer.

If You are not saved you can do so right now by believing in your heart and confessing with your mouth that Christ is Lord.

God is inviting you into a relationship with Him today!

The Salvation Prayer!

Father, it is written in Your Word that if I confess with my mouth that Jesus is Lord and believe in my heart that You have raised Him from the dead, I shall be saved.

Father, I confess that Jesus is my Lord. I make Him my Lord and Savior right now. I believe in my heart and confess with my mouth that You raised Jesus from the dead. I renounce my past life with satan and close the door to any of his devices. I thank You for forgiving all my sins through the cost of shed blood. Jesus is my Lord, and I am a new creation. Old things have passed away; now all things become new in Jesus' name. Amen.

"You shall not bow down to them or worship them; for I, the Lord your God, am a jealous God…"
Exodus 20:5

For God so loved the world that He gave His only begotten Son, that whoever believes in Him should not perish but have everlasting life.

John 3.16

WARFARE PRAYER FOR EMANCIPATION & DELIVERANCE FROM WITCHCRAFT & SPIRITUAL MANIPULATION

This prayer Goes out to every, witch doctor, every voodoo priestess, spirit of Jezebel, Judas or Baal, every demon (Church demons too), magistrates, false teachers, false preachers, principalities, soothsayer, psalmist, cohorts of the devil or evil forces of the air. Father God with this legal petition & decree; we ask that "You" herby break every bondage, curse, hex, spell, heresy, ever demonic infiltration, possession, ungodly soul tie and influence over our lives, set out to bound us to ungodly soul ties and destinies designed to sabotage the calling, plans & purposes of God. By the power of the anointing and your all so powerful Holy Ghost, devastate, destroy and demolish every enslaving yoke and oppressive chain linked to every daughter, son, church, city, government, nation, family, marriage, mind and sexuality that belongs to you, and is marked by you according to your Holy and Righteous will. Devil you got 15 seconds to evacuate the edifice. We arrest you! You are hereby bound in the name of Jesus and order you to "Get out"! Or have the Army of God carry you out. You may have come in one way but the Spirit of the Lord shall scatter you seven different ways. It ends here, it ends now, and it ends with me. For the redeemed of God is saying so. Affirmatively standing on my legal authoritative right, I am victorious through my God. I can do all things through Christ who strengthens me. I am the head and not the tail above and not beneath. I'm a child of heaven, my hope is secured because my Redeemer "liveth". It is finished. Therefore, get the behind me devil, you old defeated, tired, worthless foe, take your raggedy- face demons with you. I decree, declare, speak forth and prophesy everything spoken here that is believed by faith, is hereby done by the power of God, released through me. Working in my favor for my good. It shall be granted unto me, in Jesus' name

Time for effectual Prayer

"Spiritual Emancipation & Deliverance" from Witchcraft & Spiritual Manipulation

Heavenly father, we bow in complete surrender to you. We surrender our mind, spirit and soul to you. Let the same mind be in us that is in Christ Jesus. May the Helmet of salvation guard our thoughts, and precepts continually so that we are not deceived by the accuser of this world, that no one takes us captive through hollow and deceptive philosophies, depending on human traditions of elementary obsolete, carnal forces of this world rather than Jesus. _He who is the Christ_". We hereby repent and renounce any ungodly allegiance or association that may have opened the door to evil forces or gave way to a foot hole of the devil and his ungodly soul ties. Father, allow no spirit of darkness to manipulate our soul, take hostage our minds or hinder the destiny you have for our lives. **Jeremiah 29 11** "You know the plans you have for us, plans to prosper us and not to harm us, plans for a hope and a future". We are worthy to serve you in spirit and in truth. The power of God is mighty through the battle, for the pulling down of every stronghold of this life and to the healing of every wound. In this battle anoint our heads with fresh oil from heaven. Deliver us, from the snare and the fowler. If you be for us, it's better than the whole world against us. Jesus already showed who he was when he defeated all forces of darkness , death, hell, the grave, lake , abyss and sheol, for our name sake. We bless your Holy Name that even while we are still, you are fighting this battle for us. This battle does not belong to us but to the Lord, who reveals himself through his anointing. The anointing breaks every chain and destroys every single fetter . We take a stand against all the workings of satan that would attempt to keep our mind in bondage and or our hearts deceived. All spirits of this world are subject to Christ Jesus and bow and submit to his authority. We lift up the shield of Faith against all the fiery darts of the enemy and take a stand against the devil's scams. Every trap that the enemy sets for us will backfire on him and work out for our good. For all things work together for the good of those who love the Lord and are called according to his purpose. For the weapons of this warfare, are mighty in battle for the pulling down of strongholds, any fabrications or imaginations that exalts itself against the true knowledge of God. Jesus in our own lives we tear down the strongholds of satan against our minds and against our hearts. We bind every stronghold satan has formed against your will. We surrender your will to you and choose to honor your will, obey your commandments and follow your law. The enemy must flee. We ask that you strengthen us and enlighten us in the heavenlies, show us every way satan is tempting, lying and distorting the truth in our lives that no man deceives us. We are your workmanship by faith to bring forth all of the work of the crucifixion, resurrection, glorification and acts of Pentecost this day. Father, whatever we bind on earth is bound in heaven, whatever we loose on earth will be loosed in heaven. Jesus has given unto us power and authority to cast out demons in, His name, for even the demons tremble and believe. Therefore, we speak to satan, principalities, evil spirits, witches , warlocks, rulers of darkness, spiritual wickedness in heavenly/earthly places and the demonic lurking spirits of "Witchcraft and Spiritual Manipulation". We take authority and bind you away from **Call his/her name** We take authority over the spirits of witchcraft and spiritual manipulation for/on Behalf of **Call his/her name** in the name of the Lord Jesus Christ and command them to be Bound. Be unto us, a shield and a buckler. Stand up for our help. Fight against those that fight against us, contend with those that contend with us. Draw out your spear and destroy every enemy of our soul who pursues us for destruction. No weapon formed against us shall prosper any tongue that rises against us ,Lord, you shall condemn. Let lying tongues be put to shame, bought to dishonor and mutual confusion who assassinate our character and seek after our soul and life. I decree and declare their ways are dark and slippery with the Army of the Lord pursuing and devouring them. I plead the Blood of Jesus over my life and against any demons, curses, hexes, witchcraft prayers, accidents, catastrophes, diseases, illnesses, sicknesses that could or would possibly come against me. I decree and declare that every negative thought and enslaving yoke is hereby destroyed in Jesus' name. I have full faith and belief that the Blood of Christ will always protect me. Ministering spirits of God, go fourth before me and provide help, assistance and deliverance to **Call his/her name** in the name of Jesus. We are not ignorant of satan's devices. We resist him, he must flee. Father, you have given us Power and Authority to trample over snakes and scorpions and if bit by no means shall we be harmed. With this word of Spirit, we destroy the forces of darkness. We rebuke the lies, accusations, insinuations of the enemy. Satan, we bind you in the name and by the blood of Jesus Christ. Though we are in this world, we are not of this world. I decree and declare; we are hereby delivered from this present evil world. Delivered from the powers of darkness and translated into the kingdom of Christ Jesus. We are not slaves to anyone or anything, for whom the son sets free is free indeed. We give Satan no place in our life and only appeal to the seven Spirits of the Lord. The Spirit of the Lord. The spirit of Wisdom and Understanding, The Spirit of Counsel and Might, The Spirit of knowledge and fear of the Lord. Through the redemption of sin, we are freed from the law of sin and death. Satan's works are hereby destroyed, demolished and devastated in **Call his/her name** 's life **Call his/her name** is hereby loosed! from the enemy's evil enslaving hold; in the Name of Jesus. Always grant discernment to me in every attempt the enemy makes to frustrate the plans of God, distract our purpose or road block our prayer life. We release our lives into your all-powerful hands and ask that you find ways to release yourself through us in every area and decision of our lives. Christ covers us and satan has no right to anything that belongs to us, especially our minds. Thank you, Jesus, for intercessions. Thank You for taking your prayers before your father, Thank You! for victory and the power to overcome. I praise your Holy and Righteous name and seal this prayer in the matchless name of Jesus "he who is the Christ" our "Promised Risen Mesiah" for ever and ever. Amen!

And Jesus came and spoke to them, saying, "All authority has been given to Me in heaven and on earth. Go therefore and make disciples of all the nations, baptizing them in the name of the Father and of the Son and of the Holy Spirit, teaching them to observe all things that I have commanded you; and lo, I am with you always, even to the end of the age." Amen.
Matthew 5:13-16

" _**We should no longer be children, tossed to and fro and carried about with every wind of doctrine, by the trickery of men, in the cunning craftiness of deceitful plotting,**_ *15 but, speaking the truth in love, may grow up in all things into Him who the head—Christ…. In Him we have redemption through His blood, the forgiveness of sins, according to the riches of His grace, which He made to abound toward us in all wisdom and prudence, In Him, also we have obtained an inheritance.*"

WORKS CITED

Bible Gateway. "Be sober, be vigilant; because your adversary the devil, as a roaring lion, walketh about, seeking whom he may devour." *1 Peter 5,* n.d., *https://www.biblegateway.com/quicksearch/?quicksearch=be+sober&version=KJV*. Accessed 4 February 2023.

Bible Gateway. "Isaiah 8:19-21: New King James Version." *Assyria Will Invade the Land,* n.d., https://www.biblegateway.com/passage/?search=Isaiah%208:19-21&version=NKJV. Accessed 5 February 2023.

Bordow, Todd. "Identifying and Avoiding Spiritual manipulation." *Kingdom Kompilations,* 8 Feb. 2018, http://kingdomkompilations.com/uncategorized/identifying-avoiding-spiritual-manipulation/. Accessed 4 February 2023.

Christian Faith. "Jezebel Spirit / Queen of Heaven / Harlot Spirit / Spirit of Jezebel." *Christian Faith,* https://christian-faith.com/jezebel-spirit/. Accessed 6 February 2023.

Dexter, Geralyn. "Signs of manipulative behavior: Emotional manipulation and tactics." *Verywell Health*, 24 Feb. 2022, https://www.verywellhealth.com/manipulative-behavior-5214329. Accessed 5 February 2023.

Glassman, Thea. "6 of the most infamous cults in history." *Insider*, 7 Dec. 2018, https://www.insider.com/most-infamous-cults-in-history-2018-8. Accessed 4 February 2023.

Grondin, Charles. "Why Is Mary Called Queen of Heaven?" *Catholic Answers*, https://www.catholic.com/qa/why-is-mary-called-queen-of-heaven. Accessed 5 February 2023.

King James Bible Online. "King James Bible: Altar." *King James Version*, n.d., https://www.kingjamesbibleonline.org/Altar.php4. Accessed 5 February 2023.

Knowing Jesus. "16 Bible Verses about Being Deceived." *Knowing Jesus*, https://bible.knowing-jesus.com/topics/Being-Deceived. Accessed 6 February 2023.

Knowing Jesus. "41 Bible Verses about Idolatry." *Knowing Jesus*, https://bible.knowing-jesus.com/topics/Idolatry. Accessed 5 February 2023.

Knowing Jesus. "'Decrees' in the Bible." *Knowing Jesus*, https://bible.knowing-jesus.com/words/Decrees. Accessed 2 February 2023.

Knowing Jesus. "9 Bible Verses about Citizens, Heavenly." *Knowing Jesus*, https://bible.knowing-jesus.com/topics/Citizens,-Heavenly. Accessed 3 February 2023.

Love, Valerie. *13 Signs You're a Witch: How to Determine Conclusively Whether You're a Witch & What to Do With the Power.* Butterfly Rising Publishing, 2021, p. 18.

Love, Valerie. *13 Signs You're a Witch: How to Determine Conclusively Whether You're a Witch & What to Do With the Power.* Butterfly Rising Publishing, 2021, p. 19.

Love, Valerie. *13 Signs You're a Witch: How to Determine Conclusively Whether You're a Witch & What to Do With the Power.* Butterfly Rising Publishing, 2021, pp. 19-20.

Love, Valerie. *13 Signs You're a Witch: How to Determine Conclusively Whether You're a Witch & What to Do With the Power.* Butterfly Rising Publishing, 2021, p. 20.

Love, Valerie. *13 Signs You're a Witch: How to Determine Conclusively Whether You're a Witch & What to Do With the Power.* Butterfly Rising Publishing, 2021, p. 122.

Nelson, Thomas. *The Woman's Study Bible: Receiving God's Truth for Balance, Hope, and Transformation.* Thomas Nelson Publishing, 2017, p. 289.

Nelson, Thomas. *The Nelson Study Bible: New King James Version.* Nelson Bibles, 1997, p. 987.

Occultopedia. "Occultopedia's Secret Societies, Sects, Religions, Fellowships, Orders, Brotherhoods and

Cults Links." *Occultopedia*,
https://www.occultopedia.com/sects_cults.htm.
Accessed 3 February 2023.

Superpower Wiki. "Spiritual Force Manipulation."
Fandom,
https://powerlisting.fandom.com/wiki/Spiritual_F
orce_Manipulation. Accessed 4 February 2023.

Wikipedia contributors. "Paganism." *Wikipedia*, 6 Feb.
2023, https://en.wikipedia.org/wiki/Paganism.
Accessed 2 February 2023.

Wikipedia contributors. "Credonia Mwerinde."
Wikipedia, 7 Jan. 2023,
https://en.wikipedia.org/wiki/Credonia_Mwerinde.
Accessed 4 February 2023.

Wikipedia contributors. "Manson Family." *Wikipedia*, 3
Feb. 2023.
https://en.wikipedia.org/wiki/Manson_Family#:~:
text=The%20Manson%20Family%20(known%20a
mong,late%201960s%20and%20early%201970s.
Accessed 7 February 2023.

Worley, Win. *Curses, Soul Ties, and Binding & Loosing
(Booklet Book 5)*. WRW Publications Inc., 2017.

Zain, Mohamed. "Zimbabwean pastor arrested for
selling "tickets to heaven"." *Egypt today*, 7 July 2018,
https://www.egypttoday.com/Article/1/53528/Zi
mbabwean-pastor-arrested-for-selling-tickets-to-
heaven. Accessed 4 February 2023.

www.ingramcontent.com/pod-product-compliance
Lightning Source LLC
Chambersburg PA
CBHW030314130626
46549CB00002B/858